Hemalata Iyer, PhD
Editor

D0223567

Distance Learning: Information Access and Services for Virtual Users

Distance Learning: Information Access and Services for Virtual Users has been co-published simultaneously as *The Reference Librarian*, Number 77 2002.

The Haworth Information Press
An Imprint of The Haworth Press, Inc.

Distance Learning: Information Access and Services for Virtual Users

Distance Learning: Information Access and Services for Virtual Users has been co-published simultaneously as *The Reference Librarian*, Number 77 2002.

The Reference Librarian Monographic "Separates"

Below is a list of "separates," which in serials librarianship means a special issue simultaneously published as a special journal issue or double-issue *and* as a "separate" hardbound monograph. (This is a format which we also call a "DocuSerial.")

"Separates" are published because specialized libraries or professionals may wish to purchase a specific thematic issue by itself in a format which can be separately cataloged and shelved, as opposed to purchasing the journal on an on-going basis. Faculty members may also more easily consider a "separate" for classroom adoption.

"Separates" are carefully classified separately with the major book jobbers so that the journal tie-in can be noted on new book order slips to avoid duplicate purchasing.

You may wish to visit Haworth's Website at . . .

http://www.HaworthPress.com

. . . to search our online catalog for complete tables of contents of these separates and related publications.

You may also call 1-800-HAWORTH (outside US/Canada: 607-722-5857), or Fax 1-800-895-0582 (outside US/Canada: 607-771-0012), or e-mail at:

getinfo@haworthpressinc.com

Distance Learning: Information Access and Services for Virtual Users, edited by Hemalata Iyer, PhD (No. 77, 2002). *Addresses the challenge of providing Web-based library instructional materials in a time of ever-changing technologies.*

Helping the Difficult Library Patron: New Approaches to Examining and Resolving a Long-Standing and Ongoing Problem, edited by Kwasi Sarkodie-Mensah, PhD (No. 75/76, 2002). *"Finally! A book that fills in the information cracks not covered in library school about the ubiquitous problem patron. Required reading for public service librarians." (Cheryl LaGuardia, MLS, Head of Instructional Services for the Harvard College Library, Cambridge, Massachusetts)*

Evolution in Reference and Information Services: The Impact of the Internet, edited by Di Su, MLS (No. 74, 2001). *Helps you make the most of the changes brought to the profession by the Internet.*

Doing the Work of Reference: Practical Tips for Excelling as a Reference Librarian, edited by Celia Hales Mabry, PhD (No. 72 and 73, 2001). *"An excellent handbook for reference librarians who wish to move from novice to expert. Topical coverage is extensive and is presented by the best guides possible: practicing reference librarians." (Rebecca Watson-Boone, PhD, President, Center for the Study of Information Professionals, Inc.)*

New Technologies and Reference Services, edited by Bill Katz, PhD (No. 71, 2000). *This important book explores developing trends in publishing, information literacy in the reference environment, reference provision in adult basic and community education, searching sessions, outreach programs, locating moving image materials for multimedia development, and much more.*

Reference Services for the Adult Learner: Challenging Issues for the Traditional and Technological Era, edited by Kwasi Sarkodie-Mensah, PhD (No. 69/70, 2000). *Containing research from librarians and adult learners from the United States, Canada, and Australia, this comprehensive guide offers you strategies for teaching adult patrons that will enable them to properly use and easily locate all of the materials in your library.*

Library Outreach, Partnerships, and Distance Education: Reference Librarians at the Gateway, edited by Wendi Arant and Pixey Anne Mosley (No. 67/68, 1999). *Focuses on community outreach in libraries toward a broader public by extending services based on recent developments in information technology.*

From Past-Present to Future-Perfect: A Tribute to Charles A. Bunge and the Challenges of Contemporary Reference Service, edited by Chris D. Ferguson, PhD (No. 66, 1999). *Explore reprints of selected articles by Charles Bunge, bibliographies of his published work, and original articles that draw on Bunge's values and ideas in assessing the present and shaping the future of reference service.*

Reference Services and Media, edited by Martha Merrill, PhD (No. 65, 1999). *Gives you valuable information about various aspects of reference services and media, including changes, planning issues, and the use and impact of new technologies.*

Coming of Age in Reference Services: A Case History of the Washington State University Libraries, edited by Christy Zlatos, MSLS (No. 64, 1999). *A celebration of the perseverance, ingenuity, and talent of the librarians who have served, past and present, at the Holland Library reference desk.*

Document Delivery Services: Contrasting Views, edited by Robin Kinder, MLS (No. 63, 1999). *Reviews the planning and process of implementing document delivery in four university libraries–Miami University, University of Colorado at Denver, University of Montana at Missoula, and Purdue University Libraries.*

The Holocaust: Memories, Research, Reference, edited by Robert Hauptman, PhD, and Susan Hubbs Motin (No. 61/62, 1998). *"A wonderful resource for reference librarians, students, and teachers . . . on how to present this painful, historical event." (Ephraim Kaye, PhD, The International School for Holocaust Studies, Yad Vashem, Jerusalem)*

Electronic Resources: Use and User Behavior, edited by Hemalata Iyer, PhD (No. 60, 1998). *Covers electronic resources and their use in libraries, with emphasis on the Internet and the Geographic Information Systems (GIS).*

Philosophies of Reference Service, edited by Celia Hales Mabry (No. 59, 1997). *"Recommended reading for any manager responsible for managing reference services and hiring reference librarians in any type of library." (Charles R. Anderson, MLS, Associate Director for Public Services, King County Library System, Bellevue, Washington)*

Business Reference Services and Sources: How End Users and Librarians Work Together, edited by Katherine M. Shelfer (No. 58, 1997). *"This is an important collection of papers suitable for all business librarians. . . . Highly recommended!" (Lucy Heckman, MLS, MBA, Business and Economics Reference Librarian, St. John's University, Jamaica, New York)*

Reference Sources on the Internet: Off the Shelf and onto the Web, edited by Karen R. Diaz (No. 57, 1997). *Surf off the library shelves and onto the Internet and cut your research time in half!*

Reference Services for Archives and Manuscripts, edited by Laura B. Cohen (No. 56, 1997). *"Features stimulating and interesting essays on security in archives, ethics in the archival profession, and electronic records." ("The Year's Best Professional Reading" (1998), Library Journal)*

Career Planning and Job Searching in the Information Age, edited by Elizabeth A. Lorenzen, MLS (No. 55, 1996). *"Offers stimulating background for dealing with the issues of technology and service. . . . A reference tool to be looked at often." (The One-Person Library)*

The Roles of Reference Librarians: Today and Tomorrow, edited by Kathleen Low, MLS (No. 54, 1996). *"A great asset to all reference collections. . . . Presents important, valuable information for reference librarians as well as other library users." (Library Times International)*

Reference Services for the Unserved, edited by Fay Zipkowitz, MSLS, DA (No. 53, 1996). *"A useful tool in developing strategies to provide services to all patrons." (Science Books & Films)*

Library Instruction Revisited: Bibliographic Instruction Comes of Age, edited by Lyn Elizabeth M. Martin, MLS (No. 51/52, 1995). *"A powerful collection authored by respected practitioners who have stormed the bibliographic instruction (BI) trenches and, luckily for us, have recounted their successes and shortcomings." (The Journal of Academic Librarianship)*

Library Users and Reference Services, edited by Jo Bell Whitlatch, PhD (No. 49/50, 1995). *"Well-planned, balanced, and informative. . . . Both new and seasoned professionals will find material for service attitude formation and practical advice for the front lines of service." (Anna M. Donnelly, MS, MA, Associate Professor and Reference Librarian, St. John's University Library)*

Social Science Reference Services, edited by Pam Baxter, MLS (No. 48, 1995). *"Offers practical guidance to the reference librarian. . . . A valuable source of information about specific literatures within the social sciences and the skills and techniques needed to provide access to those literatures." (Nancy P. O'Brien, MLS, Head, Education and Social Science Library, and Professor of Library Administration, University of Illinois at Urbana-Champaign)*

Reference Services in the Humanities, edited by Judy Reynolds, MLS (No. 47, 1994). *"A well-chosen collection of situations and challenges encountered by reference librarians in the humanities." (College Research Library News)*

Racial and Ethnic Diversity in Academic Libraries: Multicultural Issues, edited by Deborah A. Curry, MLS, MA, Susan Griswold Blandy, MEd, and Lyn Elizabeth M. Martin, MLS (No. 45/46, 1994). *"The useful techniques and attractive strategies presented here will provide the incentive for fellow professionals in academic libraries around the country to go and do likewise in their own institutions." (David Cohen, Adjunct Professor of Library Science, School of Library and Information Science, Queens College; Director, EMIE (Ethnic Materials Information Exchange); Editor, EMIE Bulletin)*

School Library Reference Services in the 90s: Where We Are, Where We're Heading, edited by Carol Truett, PhD (No. 44, 1994). *"Unique and valuable to the the teacher-librarian as well as students of librarianship. . . . The overall work successfully interweaves the concept of the continuously changing role of the teacher-librarian." (Emergency Librarian)*

Reference Services Planning in the 90s, edited by Gail Z. Eckwright, MLS, and Lori M. Keenan, MLS (No. 43, 1994). *"This monograph is well-researched and definitive, encompassing reference service as practices by library and information scientists. . . . It should be required reading for all professional librarian trainees." (Feliciter)*

Librarians on the Internet: Impact on Reference Services, edited by Robin Kinder, MLS (No. 41/42, 1994). *"Succeeds in demonstrating that the Internet is becoming increasingly a challenging but practical and manageable tool in the reference librarian's ever-expanding armory." (Reference Reviews)*

Reference Service Expertise, edited by Bill Katz (No. 40, 1993). *This important volume presents a wealth of practical ideas for improving the art of reference librarianship.*

Modern Library Technology and Reference Services, edited by Samuel T. Huang, MLS, MS (No. 39, 1993). *"This book packs a surprising amount of information into a relatively few number of pages. . . . This book will answer many questions." (Science Books and Films)*

Assessment and Accountability in Reference Work, edited by Susan Griswold Blandy, Lyn M. Martin, and Mary L. Strife (No. 38, 1992). *"An important collection of well-written, real-world chapters addressing the central questions that surround performance and services in all libraries." (Library Times International)*

The Reference Librarian and Implications of Mediation, edited by M. Keith Ewing, MLS, and Robert Hauptman, MLS (No. 37, 1992). *"An excellent and thorough analysis of reference mediation. . . . Well worth reading by anyone involved in the delivery of reference services." (Fred Batt, MLS, Associate University Librarian for Public Services, California State University, Sacramento)*

Library Services for Career Planning, Job Searching and Employment Opportunities, edited by Byron Anderson, MA, MLS (No. 36, 1992). *"An interesting book which tells professional libraries how to set up career information centers. . . . Clearly valuable reading for anyone establishing a career library." (Career Opportunities News)*

In the Spirit of 1992: Access to Western European Libraries and Literature, edited by Mary M. Huston, PhD, and Maureen Pastine, MLS (No. 35, 1992). *"A valuable and practical [collection] which every subject specialist in the field would do well to consult." (Western European Specialists Section Newsletter)*

Access Services: The Convergence of Reference and Technical Services, edited by Gillian M. McCombs, ALA (No. 34, 1992). *"Deserves a wide readership among both technical and public services librarians. . . . Highly recommended for any librarian interested in how reference and technical services roles may be combined." (Library Resources & Technical Services)*

Opportunities for Reference Services: The Bright Side of Reference Services in the 1990s, edited by Bill Katz (No. 33, 1991). *"A well-deserved look at the brighter side of reference services. . . . Should be read by reference librarians and their administrators in all types of libraries." (Library Times International)*

Government Documents and Reference Services, edited by Robin Kinder, MLS (No. 32, 1991). *Discusses access possibilities and policies with regard to government information, covering such important topics as new and impending legislation, information on most frequently used and requested sources, and grant writing.*

The Reference Library User: Problems and Solutions, edited by Bill Katz (No. 31, 1991). *"Valuable information and tangible suggestions that will help us as a profession look critically at our users and decide how they are best served." (Information Technology and Libraries)*

Continuing Education of Reference Librarians, edited by Bill Katz (No. 30/31, 1990). *"Has something for everyone interested in this field. . . . Library trainers and library school teachers may well find stimulus in some of the programs outlined here." (Library Association Record)*

Weeding and Maintenance of Reference Collections, edited by Sydney J. Pierce, PhD, MLS (No. 29, 1990). *"This volume may spur you on to planned activity before lack of space dictates 'ad hoc' solutions." (New Library World)*

Serials and Reference Services, edited by Robin Kinder, MLS, and Bill Katz (No. 27/28, 1990). *"The concerns and problems discussed are those of serials and reference librarians everywhere. . . . The writing is of a high standard and the book is useful and entertaining. . . . This book can be recommended." (Library Association Record)*

Rothstein on Reference: . . . with some help from friends, edited by Bill Katz and Charles Bunge, PhD, MLS (No. 25/26, 1990). *"An important and stimulating collection of essays on reference librarianship. . . . Highly recommended!" (Richard W. Grefrath, MA, MLS, Reference Librarian, University of Nevada Library)* Dedicated to the work of Sam Rothstein, one of the world's most respected teachers of reference librarians, this special volume features his writings as well as articles written about him and his teachings by other professionals in the field.

Integrating Library Use Skills Into the General Education Curriculum, edited by Maureen Pastine, MLS, and Bill Katz (No. 24, 1989). *"All contributions are written and presented to a high standard with excellent references at the end of each. . . . One of the best summaries I have seen on this topic." (Australian Library Review)*

Expert Systems in Reference Services, edited by Christine Roysdon, MLS, and Howard D. White, PhD, MLS (No. 23, 1989). *"The single most comprehensive work on the subject of expert systems in reference service." (Information Processing and Management)*

Information Brokers and Reference Services, edited by Bill Katz and Robin Kinder, MLS (No. 22, 1989). *"An excellent tool for reference librarians and indispensable for anyone seriously considering their own information-brokering service." (Booklist)*

Information and Referral in Reference Services, edited by Marcia Stucklen Middleton, MLS, and Bill Katz (No. 21, 1988). *Investigates a wide variety of situations and models which fall under the umbrella of information and referral.*

Reference Services and Public Policy, edited by Richard Irving, MLS, and Bill Katz (No. 20, 1988). *Looks at the relationship between public policy and information and reports ways in which libraries respond to the need for public policy information.*

Finance, Budget, and Management for Reference Services, edited by Ruth A. Fraley, MLS, MBA, and Bill Katz (No. 19, 1989). *"Interesting and relevant to the current state of financial needs in reference service. . . . A must for anyone new to or already working in the reference service area." (Riverina Library Review)*

Current Trends in Information: Research and Theory, edited by Bill Katz and Robin Kinder, MLS (No. 18, 1987). *"Practical direction to improve reference services and does so in a variety of ways ranging from humorous and clever metaphoric comparisons to systematic and practical methodological descriptions." (American Reference Books Annual)*

International Aspects of Reference and Information Services, edited by Bill Katz and Ruth A. Fraley, MLS, MBA (No. 17, 1987). *"An informative collection of essays written by eminent librarians, library school staff, and others concerned with the international aspects of information work." (Library Association Record)*

Reference Services Today: From Interview to Burnout, edited by Bill Katz and Ruth A. Fraley, MLS, MBA (No. 16, 1987). *Authorities present important advice to all reference librarians on the improvement of service and the enhancement of the public image of reference services.*

The Publishing and Review of Reference Sources, edited by Bill Katz and Robin Kinder, MLS (No. 15, 1987). *"A good review of current reference reviewing and publishing trends in the United States . . . will be of interest to intending reviewers, reference librarians, and students." (Australasian College Libraries)*

Personnel Issues in Reference Services, edited by Bill Katz and Ruth Fraley, MLS, MBA (No. 14, 1986). *"Chock-full of information that can be applied to most reference settings. Recommended for libraries with active reference departments." (RQ)*

Reference Services in Archives, edited by Lucille Whalen (No. 13, 1986). *"Valuable for the insights it provides on the reference process in archives and as a source of information on the different ways of carrying out that process." (Library and Information Science Annual)*

Conflicts in Reference Services, edited by Bill Katz and Ruth A. Fraley, MLS, MBA (No. 12, 1985). *This collection examines issues pertinent to the reference department.*

Evaluation of Reference Services, edited by Bill Katz and Ruth A. Fraley, MLS, MBA (No. 11, 1985). *"A much-needed overview of the present state of the art vis-à-vis reference service evaluation. . . . Excellent. . . . Will appeal to reference professionals and aspiring students." (RQ)*

Library Instruction and Reference Services, edited by Bill Katz and Ruth A. Fraley, MLS, MBA (No. 10, 1984). *"Well written, clear, and exciting to read. This is an important work recommended for all librarians, particularly those involved in, interested in, or considering bibliographic instruction. . . . A milestone in library literature." (RQ)*

Reference Services and Technical Services: Interactions in Library Practice, edited by Gordon Stevenson and Sally Stevenson (No. 9, 1984). *"New ideas and longstanding problems are handled with humor and sensitivity as practical suggestions and new perspectives are suggested by the authors." (Information Retrieval & Library Automation)*

Reference Services for Children and Young Adults, edited by Bill Katz and Ruth A. Fraley, MLS, MBA (No. 7/8, 1983). *"Offers a well-balanced approach to reference service for children and young adults." (RQ)*

Video to Online: Reference Services in the New Technology, edited by Bill Katz and Ruth A. Fraley, MLS, MBA (No. 5/6, 1983). *"A good reference manual to have on hand. . . . Well-written, concise, provide[s] a wealth of information." (Online)*

Ethics and Reference Services, edited by Bill Katz and Ruth A. Fraley, MLS, MBA (No. 4, 1982). *Library experts discuss the major ethical and legal implications that reference librarians must take into consideration when handling sensitive inquiries about confidential material.*

Reference Services Administration and Management, edited by Bill Katz and Ruth A. Fraley, MLS, MBA (No. 3, 1982). *Librarianship experts discuss the management of the reference function in libraries and information centers, outlining the responsibilities and qualifications of reference heads.*

Reference Services in the 1980s, edited by Bill Katz (No. 1/2, 1982). *Here is a thought-provoking volume on the future of reference services in libraries, with an emphasis on the challenges and needs that have come about as a result of automation.*

Distance Learning: Information Access and Services for Virtual Users

Hemalata Iyer, PhD
Editor

Distance Learning: Information Access and Services for Virtual Users has been co-published simultaneously as *The Reference Librarian*, Number 77 2002.

The Haworth Information Press
An Imprint of
The Haworth Press, Inc.
New York • London • Oxford

Published by

The Haworth Information Press®, 10 Alice Street, Binghamton, NY 13904-1580 USA

The Haworth Information Press® is an imprint of The Haworth Press, Inc., 10 Alice Street, Binghamton, NY 13904-1580 USA.

Distance Learning: Information Access and Services for Virtual Users has been co-published simultaneously as *The Reference Librarian*, Number 77 2002.

Cover design by Jennifer M. Gaska.

Library of Congress Cataloging-in-Publication Data

Distance learning : information access and services for virtual users / Hemalata Iyer, editor.
    p. cm.
Co-published simultaneously as The reference librarian, no. 77, 2002.
Includes bibliographical references and index.
ISBN 0-7890-2052-1 (alk. paper) – ISBN 0-7890-2053-X (pbk : alk. paper)
    1. Libraries and distance education. 2. Electronic reference services (Libraries) 3. Internet in higher education. 4. Distance education. 5. Education, Higher–Effect of technological innovations on. 6. Universities and colleges–Computer networks. I. Iyer, Hemalata. II. Reference librarian.
Z718.85 .D57 2002
025.5′24–dc21
                                                                                                2002151191

Indexing, Abstracting & Website/Internet Coverage

This section provides you with a list of major indexing & abstracting services. That is to say, each service began covering this periodical during the year noted in the right column. Most Websites which are listed below have indicated that they will either post, disseminate, compile, archive, cite or alert their own Website users with research-based content from this work. (This list is as current as the copyright date of this publication.)

Abstracting, Website/Indexing Coverage . . . . Year When Coverage Began

- *Academic Abstracts/CD-ROM* 1994

- *Academic Search: data base of 2,000 selected academic serials, updated monthly: EBSCO Publishing* 1996

- *Academic Search Elite (EBSCO)* 1995

- *Academic Search Premiere (EBSCO)* 2001

- *CNPIEC Reference Guide: Chinese National Directory of Foreign Periodicals* 1995

- *Current Cites [Digital Libraries] [Electronic Publishing] [Multimedia & Hypermedia] [Networks & Networking] [General]* 2000

- *Current Index to Journals in Education* 1992

- *Educational Administration Abstracts (EAA).* 1991

- *FINDEX <www.publist.com>* 1999

- *FRANCIS. INIST/CNRS <www.inist.fr>* 1983

- *Handbook of Latin American Studies* 1999

- *IBZ International Bibliography of Periodical Literature <www.saur.de>* 1994

- *Index Guide to College Journals (core list compiled by integrating 48 indexes frequently used to support undergraduate programs in small to medium sized libraries)* 1999

(continued)

- *Index to Periodical Articles Related to Law*. 1989
- *Information Science Abstracts <www.infotoday.com>* 1989
- *Informed Librarian, The <http://www.infosourcespub.com>* 1993
- *INSPEC <www.iee.org.uk/publish/>* 1982
- *Journal of Academic Librarianship: Guide to Professional Literature, The* 1997
- *Konyvtari Figyelo (Library Review)* 1995
- *Library & Information Science Abstracts (LISA) <www.csa.com>* 1986
- *Library and Information Science Annual (LISCA) <www.lu.com>* 1997
- *Library Literature & Information Science* 1982
- *Library Reference Center (EBSCO)* 2001
- *MasterFILE: updated database from EBSCO Publishing* 1996
- *MasterFILE Elite (EBSCO)* 2001
- *MasterFILE Premier (EBSCO)* 2001
- *MasterFILE Select (EBSCO)* 2001
- *PASCAL <http://www.inist.fr>* 1983
- *Referativnyi Zhurnal (Abstracts Journal of the All-Russian Institute of Scientific and Technical Information–in Russian)*. 1993
- *Sage Public Administration Abstracts (SPAA)* 1991
- *SwetsNet <www.swetsnet.com>*. 2001

Special bibliographic notes related to special journal issues (separates) and indexing/abstracting:

- indexing/abstracting services in this list will also cover material in any "separate" that is co-published simultaneously with Haworth's special thematic journal issue or DocuSerial. Indexing/abstracting usually covers material at the article/chapter level.
- monographic co-editions are intended for either non-subscribers or libraries which intend to purchase a second copy for their circulating collections.
- monographic co-editions are reported to all jobbers/wholesalers/approval plans. The source journal is listed as the "series" to assist the prevention of duplicate purchasing in the same manner utilized for books-in-series.
- to facilitate user/access services all indexing/abstracting services are encouraged to utilize the co-indexing entry note indicated at the bottom of the first page of each article/chapter/contribution.
- this is intended to assist a library user of any reference tool (whether print, electronic, online, or CD-ROM) to locate the monographic version if the library has purchased this version but not a subscription to the source journal.
- individual articles/chapters in any Haworth publication are also available through the Haworth Document Delivery Service (HDDS).

Distance Learning: Information Access and Services for Virtual Users

CONTENTS

Introduction   1
Hemalata Iyer

The Challenges and Benefits of Asynchronous Learning Networks   3
Daphne Jorgensen

What Distance Learners Should Know About Information
   Retrieval on the World Wide Web   19
Margaret R. Garnsey

Yahoo! Do You Google? Virtual Reference Overview   31
Nancy Cannon

The Growing and Changing Role of Consortia in Providing
   Direct and Indirect Support for Distance Higher Education   39
Jane M. Subramanian

Instructional Services for Distance Education   63
Robin Kinder

Virtual Teaching: Library Instruction via the Web   71
Carol Anne Germain
Gregory Bobish

Information Literacy at Ulster County Community College:
   Going the Distance   89
Robin Walsh

Implications of Culture in Distance Education   107
Cecilia Salvatore

Assessing Outcomes with Nursing Research Assignments
and Citation Analysis of Student Bibliographies   121
   Holly Heller-Ross

Index   141

ABOUT THE EDITOR

Hemalata Iyer, PhD, is Associate Professor at the School of Information Science and Policy, University at Albany, State University of New York. Her academic interests focus on structuring and representing information, user behavior, Web-based instructional technology, cognitive aspects of retrieval, including applications of WordNet to information retrieval. Her book, *Classificatory Structures: Concepts, Relations, and Representations*, examines knowledge structures from a variety of disciplinary perspectives. She is also Editor of the book *Electronic Resources: Use and User Behavior*. Dr. Iyer teaches courses at the master's level and is also a full faculty member in the Interdisciplinary Doctoral Program in Information Science. In addition to her teaching and research, she served for several years as the U.S. Regional Coordinator for the International Society for Knowledge Organization.

Introduction

This volume centers broadly on information support services for distance education. As educators, librarians are faced with the challenge of providing Web-based, library instructional material using ever-changing technologies. Some of the challenges include assessing users' needs, developing and offering information literacy courses, employing appropriate teaching methodologies, and determining the effectiveness of the information literacy programs.

The articles herein can be categorized into two areas: access to information resources for distance learners and studies of distance learning programs. The opening article, "The Challenges and Benefits of Asynchronous Learning Networks" by Daphne Jorgensen presents the role of distance learning in education, and the overall evolution and significance of asynchronous learning networks (ALN). The paper discusses various issues in ALN, including cost, faculty and technology, learning community, social presence, and collaborative environment.

The next three articles discuss access to information resources. "What Distance Learners Should Know About Information Retrieval on the World Wide Web" by Margaret R. Garnsey finds that the Internet is a valuable information access tool for distance learners. It also examines search engines and the criteria for evaluating search results.

"Yahoo! Do You Google? Virtual Reference Overview" by Nancy Cannon provides an outline of virtual reference services encompassing electronic journal publishing, subject directories, the invisible Web, and search engines, and emphasizes the need to employ innovative ways of information delivery to serve virtual users.

The article titled "The Growing and Changing Role of Consortia in Providing Direct and Indirect Support for Distance Higher Education" by Jane M. Subramanian traces the history of consortia and cooperative efforts in facilitating user access to library resources. The paper stresses the role of consortia in supporting distance learning programs.

[Haworth co-indexing entry note]: "Introduction." Iyer, Hemalata. Co-published simultaneously in *The Reference Librarian* (The Haworth Information Press, an imprint of The Haworth Press, Inc.) No. 77, 2002, pp. 1-2; and: *Distance Learning: Information Access and Services for Virtual Users* (ed: Hemalata Iyer) The Haworth Information Press, an imprint of The Haworth Press, Inc., 2002, pp. 1-2. Single or multiple copies of this article are available for a fee from The Haworth Document Delivery Service [1-800-HAWORTH, 9:00 a.m. - 5:00 p.m. (EST). E-mail address: getinfo@haworthpressinc.com].

The next five articles present descriptions, analysis, and examples of information literacy and distance education programs. In the paper titled "Instructional Services for Distance Education," Robin Kinder presents a review of selected literature addressing user characteristics, service and staff issues involved in providing information support for distance education.

"Virtual Teaching: Library Instruction via the Web" by Carol Anne Germain and Gregory Bobish discusses the strategies, technologies, and pedagogical issues surrounding the development of Web-based library instruction tools. Topics covered include Web page design, copyright issues, Web site maintenance and usability.

Robin Walsh, in her paper titled "Information Literacy at Ulster County Community College: Going the Distance," writes about an award winning online information literacy course developed at Ulster County Community College. This course is currently offered through the SUNY Learning Network (SLN), which is a system-wide asynchronous learning network for Internet-based courses and degrees. The article traces the development of the program, outlines the course modules, and discusses the challenges of administering the program.

Cecilia Salvatore suggests that cultural factors have a bearing on the interactions and perceptions in distance education. Her article analyzes the students' journals and e-mail communications in three different classes at a Midwestern university library and information science program, and concludes that cultural issues such as community building and identity formation are central to distance education.

"Assessing Outcomes with Nursing Research Assignments and Citation Analysis of Student Bibliographies" by Holly Heller-Ross assesses the library support services provided to distance learning students in the SUNY Plattsburg Telenursing program.

It gives me pleasure to add this volume to the growing body of literature on information access and services for distance learning programs. This is a rich and exciting area of research that has both theoretical and practical implications.

Hemalata Iyer

The Challenges and Benefits
of Asynchronous Learning Networks

Daphne Jorgensen

SUMMARY. As the world has been ushered into an information age in which technology plays a major role, societal institutions have been affected on all levels. The educational institution has especially been impacted as educators, administrators, and policy makers have sought to make the most effective use of the tools of technology. One changing paradigm is the role of distance learning in education, and in particular, the evolution of asynchronous learning networks. The changing complexion of the college student population, from full-time students in their early twenties to that of more mature students who negotiate school responsibilities with those of jobs and families, justifies universities' transitioning to the asynchronous method of course delivery. Students reap the benefits in terms of convenience, but some question whether asynchronous computer-mediated learning is an effective replacement for face-to-face collaboration and if student learning is compromised with this mode of instruction. This paper will briefly discuss the cost of instituting online courses and then explore how these courses can be used to foster a rich collaborative learning environment and classroom community. *[Article copies available for a fee from The Haworth Document Delivery Service: 1-800-HAWORTH. E-mail address: <getinfo@haworthpressinc. com> Website: <http://www.HaworthPress.com> © 2002 by The Haworth Press, Inc. All rights reserved.]*

Daphne Jorgensen is a doctoral student in the School of Education, University of Albany, with a specialization in instructional technology (E-mail: daphne@nycap. rr.com).

Address correspondence to the author at: 2 Velina Drive, Albany, NY 12203.

[Haworth co-indexing entry note]: "The Challenges and Benefits of Asynchronous Learning Networks." Jorgensen, Daphne. Co-published simultaneously in *The Reference Librarian* (The Haworth Information Press, an imprint of The Haworth Press, Inc.) No. 77, 2002, pp. 3-17; and: *Distance Learning: Information Access and Services for Virtual Users* (ed: Hemalata Iyer) The Haworth Information Press, an imprint of The Haworth Press, Inc., 2002, pp. 3-17. Single or multiple copies of this article are available for a fee from The Haworth Document Delivery Service [1-800-HAWORTH, 9:00 a.m. - 5:00 p.m. (EST). E-mail address: getinfo@haworthpressinc.com].

3

KEYWORDS. Distance learning, learning networks, digital reference services, online educational courses

As the world has been ushered into an information age in which technology plays a major role, societal institutions have been affected on all levels. The educational institution has especially been impacted as educators, administrators, and policy makers have sought to make the most effective use of the tools of technology. One changing paradigm is the role of distance learning in education, and in particular, the evolution of asynchronous learning networks.

Asynchronous learning networks (ALNs) have sprung up in universities and in the private commercial sector across the world. This distance learning method (whereby students remotely access courses at their convenience using a computer with Internet access) affords students the opportunity to learn anytime, anywhere and to be involved in a community of learners, without ever leaving home. ALN offers adult learners the opportunity to take courses from prestigious universities or well-known professors without having to relocate or leave their current jobs.

Futurists predict that as this mode of education rapidly infiltrates the mainstream of higher education, it will increasingly become the trend. Many universities are embracing these networks and offering courses in both the traditional and ALN fashions. Some say those universities that do not redesign their teaching and learning environment to accommodate distance learning "will likely be among the 500 or so colleges that are predicted to go out of business in the next two decades" (Beaudoin 1998).

Given that the profile of today's college student has changed significantly from that of the past, many schools are trying to accommodate non-traditional students through computer-mediated methods of course delivery. U.S. Department of Education reports (1996 and 1997) disclosed that only one out of six American college students fit the traditional profile: that of an eighteen to twenty-two year-old who attends school full-time and lives on campus. Today, adult learners are most likely juggling their school responsibilities with families and full- or part-time jobs (54%). Additionally, today's students commute to school from far distances, with 43% attending school only part-time (Ocker & Yaverbaum 1999).

This shift in the composition of the American college population provides an impetus for change. Throughout its history, the American educational system has been in a constant state of flux. Curriculum movements emerged, impacting previous ones, and propelling leaders and ideologies forward. This trend towards implementing distance learning courses in universities is another challenge–and opportunity–in the evolution of American education (and indeed, of the world).

COST

However, as with any transition, distance education comes with a price. Some of the pitfalls encountered with ALNs include costs, tremendous demands placed on faculty members, and technology. One may ask, is this new trend worth the investment in time, effort, and finances? Do ALN courses afford students the same rich collaborative constructivist learning experiences as traditional courses in classrooms? Are student learning outcomes sacrificed on the altar of convenience? Following is a brief overview of some of the challenges encountered as universities have begun to implement this new method of course delivery.

Financial

Before adapting to an online mode of instruction, administrators must count the cost of linking geographically dispersed teachers and students. "Institutions may initially think that online courses are a 'cheap' way to deliver education. If done with attention to quality, which means that full time faculty should develop and at least be involved in conducting courses, it is actually more expensive" (Hiltz 1997). The initial cost of initiating and maintaining these networks is high. The cost of networking, setting up a platform, hiring instructional designers or course developers to work with faculty members to convert traditional courses to this format, administering the network and troubleshooting technical problems, may deter schools from making the initial investment.

A 1997 study revealed the cost effectiveness of ALNs was greater than the traditional classroom lecture method. This was due to a number of factors, including the ability to easily modify and reuse online materials. There was also qualitative evidence that a scale-up was possible. Scale-up refers to the increase in student-to-faculty ratio. Professors of online courses can actually reach more students because of the open character of computer conferencing and the ability to answer questions one time in the course and have the answer remain on the course discussion board. Based on experiments, Bourne, McMaster, Rieger, and Campbell determined that scale-up was possible as follows: a class of 83, one instructor, two teaching assistants, 2 graders, and 25 remote mentors. This group believed the same teaching complement could support a class of up to 150 students (Bourne, McMaster, Rieger, and Campbell, 1997).

This translates into cost savings. However, note the remote mentors in the above experiment are unpaid, so this scenario is really contingent upon the continued goodwill of volunteers. Technology and networking costs, and the professional people needed to support the system, also translate into big bucks. One wonders if schools will merely take money out of one category (i.e., full time faculty) and shift it to another (i.e., networking costs).

That leads to another challenge as schools are hopping onto the distance education bandwagon: faculty.

Faculty Investment

Faculty members are big stakeholders in this new trend towards ALNs. They have a lot to gain and a lot to lose as universities hire more adjunct professors from remote locations in lieu of full time faculty in order to effect the cost savings mentioned above. Some of the challenges for faculty members include:

- Increased workload and more start-up time in order to fully prepare courses (videos or online materials, Website, etc.) before the semester (Hiltz 1997).
- The instructor adapts a new role as facilitator: instead of the sage on the stage, he is the "guide on the side" (Rossman 1999). Teachers may have difficulty adapting to this guide model due to long familiarity with the traditional "sage" model (Bourne, McMaster Rieger, and Campbell 1997).
- Completely rethink their courses and adapt a whole new approach with a whole new medium for course delivery. This is not merely a matter of simply transferring course content to various media (i.e., sage on the stage becomes "sage in the box") (Bourne 1997), but rather to *redesign the whole course* in order to effectively flow in the new media.
- Increased need for organizational skills as faculty members must grade and post assignments differently than in the face-to-face mode (Hilz 1997).
- Instructor's role as "cybernet cowboy" trying to round up the students the first couple of weeks of school (out of sight, out of mind, as students focus more attention on the courses they physically attend) (Hilz 1997).
- Faculty training on using collaborative learning approaches (Hilz 1997).
- Faculty technical training.
- The level of communication with students is more demanding as faculty need to provide constant feedback to students in an ALN mode (Rossman 1997). Also, communication needs to be very clear and consistent.
- After all the work faculty members put into developing new courses for the ALN mode, there is still some debate about who actually owns those courses.
- Another debate is the issue of compensation as faculty members invest much time in between semesters preparing for their courses (Hilz 1997).

Technology

ALNs are dependent on computers and networks. " 'Bits (0s and 1s), which are the DNA of information,' are rapidly replacing atoms as the 'basic commodity of human interaction' " (Nicholas Negroponte, as qtd. in Cyrs 1997). Hence, in this computer-mediated instruction forum, the computer is used as a tool to connect not only information, but humans. In ALNs the academic culture becomes more contingent on the computer as mediator. This can sometimes be frustrating and expensive when technical problems ensue.

Other challenges of ALN course delivery include a higher drop-out rate than traditional classes, a tendency for more students to procrastinate and fall behind in their assignments than in traditional classes, and difficulty in developing close personal friendships. Hilz (1997) found in her virtual classroom course that only one third of the students had formed close friendships, whereas in traditional courses, most students do.

In spite of these challenges, proponents of ALNs assert that this mode of instruction actually enhances the academic community and fosters a rich collaborative atmosphere that is student-centered. The interaction between professor and student, and peer-to-peer, foster a learning community. Most of the challenges to this mode of course delivery seem to be technical and logistical, but certainly not insurmountable. They are "growing pains" to this transition in education.

COLLABORATIVE LEARNING ENVIRONMENT

The underlying premise in a collaborative learning environment is that the learner actively participates in the co-construction of knowledge. This Vygotskian constructivism is drawn from the theory of situated learning or situated cognition where learning occurs in a sociocultural context. As learners are immersed in the learning context, they construct knowledge in transaction with their environment, internalizing key concepts, and in the process both are changed (Airasian & Walsh 1997; Semple 2000). This is also in keeping with cognitive apprenticeship theory of instruction that "embeds the learning of skills and knowledge in their social and functional context" (Collins, Brown & Newman 1989).

Accordingly, learning is a social and cultural phenomenon as much as it is a cognitive one (Vygotsky 1986; Bruner 1996). Bruner (1996) says that culture is important because education and culture are intertwined: learning happens in a cultural setting and is dependent upon the resources and tools of the culture, its traditions, and codes. Learning and thinking within the cultural setting enables people to organize and understand their world. The maxim that "no man is an island" applies to education: learning happens with other people and in a cultural framework.

Through collaborative interaction, learners participate in a community of practice. They negotiate meaning together and develop the skills to discover rich and productive solutions to problems. The critical thinking skills that are honed through social interaction prepare students for authentic real-world situations in professional work environments. This is because learning how to be a viable team member prepares students to successfully participate in professional coalitions, projects and teams (Ehrmann & Collins 2001; Borthick & Jones 2000).

The traditional face-to-face mode of instruction has been the norm for collaborative experiences but the integration of technology into the learning community has expanded the possibilities for collaboration (Ocker & Yaverbaum 1999). However, the mode of collaboration in an online classroom may be very different than that of a face-to-face class as students "do not initially know one another's assumptions, cultures, or personality quirks" and must find ways to bridge the cultural gap (Ehrmann & Collins 2001). The removal of time and space barriers affords online students the opportunity for deeper reflection and facilitates debate of issues and clarification of concepts (Hiltz 1987). On the other hand, the lack of nonverbal cues that are inherent in face-to-face communication can lead to a diminished sense of social presence or feelings of depersonalization which may translate into less effort for some members of the class. Additionally, coordinating the group work in an online class (i.e., how often and when) can sometimes be difficult (Ocker & Yaverbaum 1999).

In spite of the challenges, the online learning environment is a fertile field for deep reflection, critical evaluation of course content, and the sharing of resources among students (Palloff and Pratt 1999, 82). This environment is ideal for the development of collaborative skills as "students learn to work with and depend on each other to reach their learning objectives" (Palloff and Pratt 1999). These interpersonal interactions are a powerful catalyst for strengthening learning outcomes as knowledge is actively created in the learning community.

Hilz holds that the online classroom environment was designed to foster collaborative learning "among students, between students and instructors, among teachers, and between a class and wider academic and nonacademic communities." In a 1997 survey, students who had completed an online course compared their experience to a traditional classroom course. Hilz found that collaborative learning took place and positively affected student motivation and learning: "55% of the students felt more motivated to work hard on their assignments because other students would be reading them" (Hilz 1997). This was followed up by a three-year longitudinal study of 26 courses that compared the process and learning outcomes of asynchronous courses with those of their traditional counterparts. An imbedded field experiment explored "the separate and joint effects of working online versus in the classroom and of working individually versus in groups. The results support the premise that when students are actively involved in collaborative (group) learning online, the outcomes can be as good as or better than those for traditional classes, but when individuals are simply receiving posted material and sending back individual work, the results are poorer than in traditional classrooms" (Hilz 1999).

Palloff and Pratt (1999) maintain that the failure of many online programs has been the inability to facilitate a collaborative learning process. They suggest that other forms of collaboration can be achieved in the online forum, such as intergroup collaboration where one class prepares a project to be viewed by another class and vice versa, and that this will enhance learning. To encourage this collaboration, educators must build collaboration into the value systems of the course. Bourne et al. (1997) give extra credit to students who help other students. Students in ALN courses can interact with other students from geographically dispersed locations and exchange many perspectives about a specific field of knowledge. The intermingling of diverse cultural experiences can make an enriching contribution to the class community. As students reflect on the class discussion, they can analyze some of their own perceptions, and reconstruct their thinking on various issues. This brings to mind the concept of literate thinking. According to Bangert-Drowns and Pyke (2001), literate thinking is the highest form of learning engagement. When someone is engaged in literating thinking, he "explores alternative interpretations as an opportunity to reflect on personal values and experiences." While one is engaging in literate thinking, doors are opening to new ways of understanding things as his understanding evolves.

Collaborative learning is not only mediated by the computer, but by language. Aggarwal calls the language "linguistic acts." Linguistic acts "function as social interaction mechanisms building up collaborative learning processes" (Aggarwal 2000). Bruner discusses the importance of written language in the learning process. He cited *World on Paper* in which Olson "reviews and reflects upon the impact of literacy in Western culture. Print affects profoundly how and what we go about remembering–if only by virtue of preserving a text, a prosthetic substitute for rote memory" (Bruner 1996). In an ALN discussion forum, language is crucial to learning, to collaboration, and to the community spirit.

COMMUNITY

The building of a class community, an intimate class culture, is an essential prerequisite for successful collaboration in an online course. After all, if people do not feel "unified" why would they want to work together? As students learn from each other in a non-threatening and sympathetic environment "they develop a common sense of purpose, including a common way of thinking about how work gets done and what is necessary to accomplish a task" (Borthick & Jones 2000). This fosters a team spirit. On the other hand, without this feeling of community, people feel isolated and are "likely to be anxious, defensive, and unwilling to take the risks involved in learning" (Wegerif 1998, 48). "Notions of community are fairly elusive, but they tend to encompass qualities of relationships; shared tasks; a sense of 'self' in relation to 'other'; interdependence; and belonging" (Davis 1997). The literature has addressed a number of factors associated with successful online community building, including students taking responsibility for their learning; adequate access to the course; instructional immediacy; instructional role change; peer immediacy; social presence; discussion; and overcoming conflict.

Students Need to Be Responsible for Their Learning

"A review of the literature regarding online learning indicated that students became more involved and responsible for their participation when the entire course was not instructor driven" (Cifuentes et al. 1997; Rohfeld & Hienstra 1995, as qtd. in Poole 2000). This prompted Poole (2000) to conduct a combined qualitative and quantitative study examining the nature of student participation in an online course. The WebCT software was the platform for course delivery, and collaboration and discussion were employed in course design. Students actively participated in the class. They were required to post 27 messages during the course, but the average post per student was 73 messages. Additionally, students took turns moderating the class discussions. Some of the questions addressed in the study included: how students participated during the week they moderated the bulletin board discussion; the contents of the student's discussion postings; and how student participation contributed to the class as a community of learners.

Poole's findings supported the literature as both the number and length of discussion postings dramatically (i.e., significantly) increased for each student in the weeks in which they moderated the class discussion. Moderators posted an average of 14.5 messages during their week, whereas the average posts per student on the weeks they did not moderate was 4.76 messages [highly significant: $t = 4.261$, p less than .0011, df = 13]. Moderator postings were also longer during the week of their duties [significant: $t = 5.019$, p less than .0003, df = 13]. Poole postulates that moderating may have contributed to the students' sense of community since it was a common experience. [This is an assumption. There is no measure connected with this statement.]

Access

In an ethnographic study employing various methods to show how social factors impacted student learning, Wegerif (1998) found that in order to construct a sense of community in an asynchronous online course, students must "cross a threshold from feeling like outsiders to feeling like insiders" (Wegerif 1998). One student who had limited access from work felt as though he was an outsider to "an in group of people with almost unlimited access and that he could not be part of it for technical and practical reasons" (Wegerif 1998, 30). Two other students in his class felt the same way.

In the Poole study, students primarily accessed the course from home (74%). Students who did not have Internet access at home contributed less frequently to the class discussions and felt like outsiders to the group. This lack of access also inhibits the length of time students can be engaged with the course materials. Poole (2000) maintains "home computers are almost a necessity for students to participate" in an online course. This seems a reasonable opinion. After all, who takes a face-to-face course without pen and paper? Students need the appropriate tools with which to work. It is implicit in an online course that the tool for the course, the medium by which to communicate, is a computer with Internet access. Perhaps, though, this is a simplistic argument and opens up questions of inequities of access and social status.

Instructional Immediacy

Instructional immediacy encompasses the "nonverbal behaviors that reduce physical and/or psychological distance between teachers and students" (Andersen 1979, as qtd. in Rourke 1999). In a survey of 1,406 online students of the SUNY Learning Network, an asynchronous learning network, Swan et al. (2000) found that "an instructor who interacts frequently and constructively with students" was integral to the building of a successful online community (Swan et al. 2000). Student-teacher interaction significantly affected students' perceived learning ($p < .01$) as well as their overall satisfaction ($p < .01$) with their courses. "Students who reported low levels of interaction with their instructors also reported the lowest levels of satisfaction with their courses and the lowest levels of learning. Conversely, students who reported high levels of interaction with their instructors also reported higher levels of satisfaction with their courses and higher levels of learning from them" (Swan 2000). This indicates instructors should provide sufficient opportunity with which to interact with their students in the online forum. This finding was punctuated by an example from Open University where the success or failure of students was related to whether or not they felt like they were part of a community.

Some behaviors that augment instructional immediacy include teacher narratives about out-of-class experiences, humor, affirmative comments and praise of students, and using students' first names. These all serve to bridge the virtual gap and foster a warm and open community (Rourke 1999; LaRose 2000).

Instructor Role Change: Facilitator

Students are more proactive in electronic conversation than they are in the face-to-face classroom. Poole (2000) coded the verbal interactions according to the pedagogical moves introduced by Bellack, Kliebard, Hyman, and Smith (1966, as outlined in Poole 2000). These moves categorize four specific kinds of classroom interactions: structuring (setting the context); soliciting (verbal prompts, e.g., questions); responding (e.g., answering a question); and reacting (to all of the above, and includes "clarifying, synthesis and expanding on ideas"). Poole's graduate students performed 70.4% of the pedagogical moves while the instructor performed only 29.6%. This is indicative that the role of instructor is changing: more of a guide on the side instead of sage on the stage–a facilitator.

Peer Immediacy

Likewise, high levels of peer interaction produced higher levels of course satisfaction and high levels of perceived learning in students (Swan 2000). Wegerif found that in order for students to feel a sense of community, they had to cross an invisible barrier that ushered them in from the status of outsider to that of insider. "This threshold is essentially a social one; it is the line between feeling part of a community and feeling that one is outside that community looking in" (Wegerif 1998).

Of eleven students who responded to an end of course questionnaire seven mentioned collaborating with other students in response to, "What did you like most about the course?" (Wegerif 1998). One student felt that collaborative learning had not been effective for him, but he admitted he did not log on enough. In this same study, a student who contributed 79 discussion postings (of a high of 122) was very satisfied with the collaborative learning, while another student who only made 4 postings, was not. So the problem was not necessarily the medium, but rather that those who were contributing less were not as *involved* as they could have been. In order to collaborate (or be *involved*) in a face-to-face setting, one has to show up. Students must show up in an online environment in order to reap the benefits of the collaborative learning that is taking place there.

Social Presence

Schrum (1997) refers to the online interaction among students and faculty as "interlational" because the ALN does not just bridge geographic distance but social distance. The challenge of overcoming the face-to-face problem in an online community has been addressed in the concept of "social presence." Social presence is the feeling of face-to-face contact in a digital world and is an integral part of the establishment of community in an asynchronous classroom. Social presence is the ability of students to "project themselves socially and affectively into a community of inquiry" and has at its root "Mehrabian's 'concept of immediacy,' which he defined as 'those communication behaviors that enhance closeness to and nonverbal interaction with another'" (Rourke 1999).

Things like facial expressions, body language, and eye contact express social presence in the physical realm. Practices that foster the development of social presence in the virtual classroom include addressing class members by name (Rourke 1999; Poole 2000), expressions of feeling, self-introductions, humor, talking about outside experiences, compliments, reinforcement, encouraging words, and using emoticons (i.e., a smiley face as opposed to hearing a real voice laugh) to express emotion or to lighten the tone of the messages (Poole 2000).

Discussion

A major bridge to online social presence is the class discussions. An active dynamic discussion component that was both valued (in the grading system) and authentic was found to be integral to the success of asynchronous courses. In virtual class discussions, the professor acts like a gentle guide, facilitating the flow of discussion rather than being at its forefront: The conversation component to discussion, the dialogue, "carries a flow of meaning between participants" (Palloff 1999). It is in this class dialogue that students are receptive to the idea of restructuring their mental models. As they interact with each other, reflect on classmates' perceptions, and form their own responses, the learning community is nurtured and developed.

Expressions of warmth, congeniality, appreciation, playfulness, personal feelings (including timidity, frustration and hesitation) augment "relational solidarity to build community" (Herrman 1998, 18). Often a class culture emerges whereby people use the language of the class to foster community (e.g., insider jokes).

Friction

Poole (2000) found that a 3-week period of disagreement involving a passionate discussion of gender-related social issues that trasnscended technology, actually fostered the class sense of community–after the issue was resolved. The successful resolution of a controversial discussion in which people respectfully disagreed "created a stronger bond between meaning and understanding with each other."

In a five-year ethnographic study of an academic listserv comprised of professors, students and other psychology professionals, Herrmann (1998) explored some patterns of communication integral to community building in online environments. Methodology included participant observation (from lurking to active posting); interviews (via telephone, e-mail and face-to-face), and an online survey. "Altogether, 200 400K diskettes and one 35MB tape of messages containing a record of online communication" (Herrmann 1998) were collected and analyzed. Findings demonstrated that "communication such as naming the community, civil uses of language and conflict resolution are important factors needed to create, build, and sustain community over an extended period of time" (Herrmann 1998). Herrmann (1998) found that one period of intense discord in the listserv almost disbanded the listserv altogether. (Interestingly, this was also instigated by a gender argument related to why no female speakers were invited to a conference on "the social world.") The flaming escalated with people taking sides until the threat of eliminating the community forced them to "resolve the conflict by reclaiming responsibility and ownership" of the list.

Kanuka and Anderson (1998) used the Gunawardena, Lowe, and Anderson (Gunawardena 1997) interaction analysis model to perform content analysis on a 3-week online forum. The asynchronous discussion employed the Caucus computer conferencing system, which topically organized messages. The 252 discussion postings addressed the policy and practice of management in workplace learning centers. Methodology included an online survey, transcript analysis, and a stratified sample for a telephone survey. One of the findings directly related to the building of community was that social discord sometimes served as a catalyst for knowledge construction in an online forum (Kanuka 1998). When there were contradictory or inconsistent ideas or information posted, people would either ignore them or confront them head on. When new ideas contradicted prior established assumptions, tension occurred in the group. When this discord was directly confronted, it resulted in a "change of new paradigm structure" as people negotiated inconsistencies and embraced multiple perspectives.

CLOSING

In spite of the pitfalls or challenges of asynchronous learning networks, I am persuaded their benefits supersede their disadvantages. ALN courses, when properly prepared, offer students a rich learning environment. Properly prepared means that universities weigh the cost of implementing these courses, consider the technical training needed and the consequences this new method of course delivery will have for employees, as well as include faculty members in the decision making process. Properly prepared also means that instructors modify the course delivery to fit the medium.

It is unfortunate that much of the burden of implementing these courses falls on faculty members. I do believe, though, that this mode of instruction can offer a great deal to students. I do not believe that the traditional classroom method of instruction should be entirely replaced by online courses because people do have different learning styles and needs. ALN is just one way to accommodate some students. Mature adult learners tend to work well in this environment and show persistence in completing their course work. However, ALN courses are not for everyone. For instance, young college students may truly need the face-to-face social structure found in the traditional university setting. For them, the social presence in the online forum may not be enough.

I believe ALNs can foster a rich collaborative learning environment and a sense of community. The project-oriented approach to online learning helps with that, as students are encouraged to work together and share resources with one another. Discussion is a crucial element to building community, as well as to the fostering of social presence in this environment. I believe ALNs are still in a formative stage and that the potential for building online collaboration and real community needs to be explored and illuminated further.

REFERENCES

Aggarwal, A. (2000). *Web-based learning and teaching technologies: Opportunities and challenge.* Hershey, USA: Idea Group Publishing, 227.

Airasian, P. W. & Walsh, M. E. (1997). "Cautions for classroom constructivists." *Education Digest* 62(8): 62-69.

Bangert-Drowns, R. L. & Pyke, C. (2001). "Student engagement with educational software: An exploration of literate thinking with electronic literature." *Journal of Educational Computing Research* 24(3), 213-234.

Beaudoin, M. F. (1998). "A new professoriate for the new millenium." *DEOS News*, 8(5), Editorial. ISSN: 1062-9416.

Borthick, A. F. & Jones, D. R. (2000). "The motivation for collaborative discovery learning online and its application in an information systems assurance course." *Issues in Accounting Education* 15(2): 181-211.

Bourne, J. R. et al. (1997). "Paradigms for on-line learning: A case study in the design and implementation of an asynchronous learning networks (ALN) course." *Journal of Asynchronous Learning Networks.* (Vol. 1(2)-Aug.). Retrieved March 14, 2001 from the World Wide Web: http://www.aln.org/alnweb/journal/issue2/assee.htm.

Bruner, Jerome. (1996). *The culture of education.* Cambridge, MA: Harvard University Press.

Collins, A., Brown, J. S., Newman, S. E. (1989). "Cognitive apprenticeship: Teaching the crafts of reading, writing, and mathematics." In Resnick, L. B. & Glaser, R. (Ed.). *Knowing, learning, and instruction: Essays in honor of Robert Glaser.* (pp. 453-494). Hillsdale, NJ: Lawrence Erlbaum Associates, Inc.

Cyrs, T. E. (1997). *Teaching and learning at a distance: What it takes to effectively design, deliver, and evaluate programs* (71 Fall 1997). San Francisco, CA: Jossey-Bass Publishers.

Davis, M. (1997) "Fragmented by technologies: A community in cyberspace." *Interpersonal Computing and Technology* 5(1-2): 7-18. ISSN: 1064-4326. Retrieved November 10, 2001 from the World Wide Web: http://jan.ucc.nau.edu/~ipct-j/1997/n2/davis.html.

Ehrmann, S. C. & Collins, M. (2001). "Emerging models of online collaborative learning: Can distance enhance quality?" *Educational Technology* (September-October 2001): 34-38.

Gunawardena, C. N., Lowe, C. A., Anderson, T. (1997). "Analysis of a global online debate and the development of an interaction analysis model for examining social construction of knowledge in computer conferencing." *Journal of Educational Computing Research 17*(4): 397-431.

Herrmann, F. (1998). "Building on-line communities of practice: An example and implications." *Educational Technology* (January-February 1998): 16-23.

Hiltz, S. R. (1997). "Impacts of college-level courses via asynchrnous learning networks: Some preliminary results." *Journal of Asynchronous Learning Networks.* Retrieved February 7, 2001 from the World Wide Web: http:eies.njit.edu/~hiltz/workingpapers/philly/philly.htm.

Hiltz, S. R. (1999). "Measuring the importance of collaborative learning for the effectiveness of ALN: A multi-measure, multi-method approach." Retrieved March 19, 2001 from the World Wide Web: http://www.aln.org/alnweb/journal/Vol4_issue2/le/hiltz/le-hiltz.htm.

Kanuka, H., Anderson, T. (1998). "Online social interchange, discord, and knowledge construction." *Journal of Distance Education 13*(1): [iuicode: http://www.icaap.org/iuicode?151.13.1.5].

LaRose, R. & Whitten, P. (2000). "Re-thinking instructional immediacy for web courses: A social cognitive exploration." *Communication Education 49*(4): 320-338.

Ocker, Rosalie, J. & Yaverbaum, Gayle J. (1999). "Asynchronous computer-mediated communication versus face-to-face collaboration: Results on student learning, quality and satisfaction." *Group Decision and Negotiation 8*: 427-440.

Palloff, R. M. & Pratt, K. (1999). *Building learning communities in cyberspace: Effective strategies for the online classroom.* San Francisco, CA: Jossey-Bass, Inc.

Poole, D. M. (2000). "Student participation in a discussion-oriented online course: A case study." *Journal of Research on Computing in Education 33*(2): 162, 16p, 7 charts.

Rourke, L., Anderson, T., Garrison, D., & Archer, W. (1999). "Assessing social presence in asynchronous text-based computer conferencing." *Journal of Distance Education 14*(2): [iuicode: http://www.icaap.org/iuicode?151.14.2.6].

Rossman, M. H. (1999). "Successful online teaching using an asynchronous learning discussion forum." *Journal of Asynchronous Learning Networks.* (Vol. 3(2)-Nov.). Retrieved from the World Wide Web on November 28, 2000: http://www.aln.org/alnweb/journal/Vol3_issue2/Rossman.htm.

Schrum, L. & Berenfeld, B. (1997). *Teaching and learning in the information age: A guide to educational telecommunications.* Boston, Massachusetts: Allyn & Bacon.

Semple, A. (2000). "Learning theories and their influence on the development and use of educational technologies." *Australian Science Teachers Journal* 46(3): 21-28.

Swan, K., Shea, P., Fredericksen, E., Pelz, W., Maher, G. (2000). "Building knowledge building communities: Consistency, contact & communication in the virtual classroom." *Journal of Educational Computing Research* 23(4): 359-83.

Vygotsky, Lev. (1986). *Thought and language.* Cambridge, MA: Massachusetts Institute of Technology.

Wegerif, R. (1998). "The social dimension of asynchronous learning networks." *Journal of Asynchronous Learning Networks* 2(1): 34-49.

What Distance Learners Should Know About Information Retrieval on the World Wide Web

Margaret R. Garnsey

SUMMARY. The Internet can be a valuable tool allowing distance learners to access information not available locally. Search engines are the most common means of locating relevant information on the Internet, but to use them efficiently students should be taught the basics of searching and how to evaluate the results. This article briefly reviews how search engines work, studies comparing search engines, and criteria useful in evaluating the quality of returned Web pages. Research indicates there are statistical differences in the precision of search engines, with AltaVista ranking high in several studies. When evaluating the quality of Web pages, standard criteria used in evaluating print resources is appropriate, as well as additional criteria which relate to the Web site itself. Giving distance learners training in how to use search engines and how to evaluate the results will allow them to access relevant information efficiently while ensuring that it is of adequate quality. *[Article copies available for a fee from The Haworth Document Delivery Service: 1-800-HAWORTH. E-mail address: <getinfo@haworthpressinc.com> Website: <http://www. HaworthPress.com> © 2002 by The Haworth Press, Inc. All rights reserved.]*

KEYWORDS. Distance learning, search engines, Web sites, evaluation methods

Margaret R. Garnsey is Assistant Professor, Business Division, Siena College, 515 Loudon Road, Loudonville, NY 12211-1462 (E-mail: garnsey@siena.edu).

[Haworth co-indexing entry note]: "What Distance Learners Should Know About Information Retrieval on the World Wide Web." Garnsey, Margaret R. Co-published simultaneously in *The Reference Librarian* (The Haworth Information Press, an imprint of The Haworth Press, Inc.) No. 77, 2002, pp. 19-30; and: *Distance Learning: Information Access and Services for Virtual Users* (ed: Hemalata Iyer) The Haworth Information Press, an imprint of The Haworth Press, Inc., 2002, pp. 19-30. Single or multiple copies of this article are available for a fee from The Haworth Document Delivery Service [1-800-HAWORTH, 9:00 a.m. - 5:00 p.m. (EST). E-mail address: getinfo@haworthpressinc.com].

INTRODUCTION

As multimedia and communication technologies have improved, the delivery of distance learning courses via the World Wide Web has increased dramatically (Lau, 2000). The Web provides a convenient way to distribute course information as well as expanded opportunities to access worldwide resources. This access is especially valuable for students in sparsely populated communities where distance learning is in great demand. While most academic libraries provide remote access to materials, the Internet can be a rich source of additional reliable, authoritative information (O'Leary, 2000).

Many students may not be familiar with efficiently finding information on the Internet, since distance learners are on average several years older than the traditional on-campus student (Johnson, 1999) and Web search engines, the most common means of finding information, did not come into existence until 1994. In addition, unlike traditional sources of information, books and journals, the Internet is a self-publishing medium. As such, for the most part, it is without editors and fact checkers who monitor and assure quality (Tate & Alexander, 1996). This allows anyone to distribute information "without regard to accuracy, validity, or bias" (Oliver, Wilkinson, & Bennett, 1997). A 1995 analysis of randomly selected Websites found 21.9% of the material was public relations and 20.7% was advertising (Wilkinson, Bennett, & Oliver, 1997). It is important that students be given training to effectively use this technology since "student support services are generally the greatest predictor of the success of a distance learning program" (Hill, 1998).

In recent years much research has been devoted to developing criteria for evaluating Internet resources. There have been two main aspects of this research: (1) development of criteria to be used in the evaluation of resources and (2) evaluation of the technology which retrieves Web pages for the Internet user. Both of these aspects are important to distance learning students. They must be able to find relevant information and once found evaluate its reliability. This paper reviews the current research in these areas.

FINDING INFORMATION ON THE INTERNET

About 800 million documents are currently thought to be on the Web (Sullivan, 1999b). People use two major types of tools to access required information. The first type, directories, deal with classificatory schemes (Liu, 1996). The second are generally referred to as "search engines." This paper confines itself to search engines since they are the most frequently used tool in finding information on the Internet.

All search engines have three major elements:

1. A spider or crawler which visits Websites and follows the links within each site. Their main functions are to index Web documents and to check for invalid links.
2. The index which contains a copy of every page the spider finds.
3. The agent which goes through the index when a query is made to find matches and to rank those matches according to perceived relevance.

Each search engine implements these elements in slightly different ways.

The largest search engines index, at most, about one-third of Web documents (Lehnert, 1998). For example, the number of Web pages indexed by some popular search engines are as follows (Sullivan, 1999a):

Self-Reported Size

Infoseek	~30 million
Google	~60 million
NorthernLight	~120 million
AltaVista	~150 million

There are several reasons for this incomplete indexing. If Web pages are isolated, meaning they are not referenced by other Web pages, they are often excluded by search engines. In addition, technical obstacles such as frames, image maps or dynamically created Websites limit the ability to index items (Sullivan, 1999a). More importantly, portions of the Web are deliberately ignored by some search engines due to the limitations of their current hardware.

Another complicating factor is that each search engine indexes different Web pages. Lawrence and Giles (1998) estimated the overlap of the top six search engines to be only around 60%. Gordon and Pathak (1999), in their study of search engines, found approximately 93% of the top-ranked documents were retrieved by only one of the eight search engines they were using. Students need to be made aware that, in order to get adequate results for some types of research, several search engines should be used. One way to assist in doing this is through the use of meta-search engines. These engines search using several different search engines at once. Many of them integrate the results from the different engines, eliminate duplicates, and sort the returned pages by a relevancy algorithm. "They (meta-search engines) should often be the engine of first resort for . . . Web searches" (Garman, 1999). However, these engines also have drawbacks. They are not able to take advantage of all the features of the individual engines, such as Boolean searches. In addition, they do not conduct exhaustive searches, often using only the top 10 to 100 hits from each engine (Liu, 1998). Therefore, while they are a good starting point, individual search engines must be consulted to get thorough results.

When using different search engines one must be aware of the special syntax that is required. For example, some search engines (ex: Infoseek) automatically truncate the terms entered, some (ex: HotBot) allow truncation, generally by following the word stem with an asterisk, and others (ex: Lycos) have no capacity for truncation. Another common example of the differences between engines is how searches involving multiple terms are treated. Some engines (ex: Exite) use OR as the default, meaning only one of the terms entered may appear in the Websites returned, while others (ex: Google) use AND as the default, meaning all of the terms entered appear. To exclude a term, some engines use a minus sign preceding the term, others NOT, and some AND NOT. Several studies have reviewed the various features available on the different search engines. Martinez and Sanchez (1999) compared the features offered by the ten most popular search engines/directories. Five of the engines ranked between 10.5 and 11.5 while NorthernLight at 13 ranked the highest by offering the most options in searching and Nerdworld at 2 offered the fewest. NorthernLight's higher rating is due, for the most part, to its extensive ability to search by fields. In order for distance learners to have success searching for information on the Web, they should be provided with instruction on the way search engines work, some of the differences between popular search engines, and methods that can be used to increase the odds of obtaining satisfactory results.

EVALUATING INTERNET SEARCH ENGINES

Since their appearance in 1994, several studies have been done comparing various search engines. They may be grouped into three categories: review of functions of different engines (like the one mentioned in the previous section), evaluative comments with simple searches, and actual tests with data collection and analysis. This section will review some of the studies which involved actual tests comparing search engines.

Gordon and Pathak (1999) tested seven search engines and one subject directory (Yahoo) using actual questions of users and having the users evaluate the relevance of the returned documents. The users were asked to describe an information need, identify the most important words or phrases in their description, identify any synonyms or related terms they thought would be helpful, and phrase their search in the form of a Boolean query. Experienced searchers, with a strong background in the Internet and the use of search engines, optimized the queries for each search engine over several iterations and the top twenty results from the best search for each engine were printed for evaluation. The printed Web pages were arranged in random order and given to the users for evaluation using a four point scale (*highly relevant, somewhat relevant, somewhat irrelevant,* or *highly irrelevant*). Using the standard IR measures of recall and precision, they concluded that the absolute retrieval effectiveness of search engines is fairly low but there were statistical differences among search engines. Statistical results indicated that AltaVista and OpenText were the best performers with HotBot and Yahoo being the worst.

Hsieh-Yee (1998) evaluated eight search engines using twenty-one actual reference questions and five made-up subject questions. Four searchers were used and each question was searched twice on each engine being evaluated. The searchers were given key terms and basic parameters on how each search engine was to be searched. The searchers used their judgment in assessing the relevance of the first ten retrieved items. Four variables: precision, duplicate, most-relevant-item, and relevancy-ranking, were used to assess the search engines. A statistical difference was found in the results from the two types of question. Therefore, the engines were evaluated separately for each question type. The best performer for reference questions was OpenText, having the top score for three of the four performance measures. For subject questions, Infoseek (now part of Go Network) was the best performer. Overall the search engines performed significantly better for the subject questions than they did for the reference questions.

Feldman (1998) compared information found on the WWW using search engines to two traditional search services, DIALOG and Dow Jones Interactive. Professional searchers, with at least two years of experience on the traditional system they were using, were used to retrieve results for real user questions. The users were then asked to rank the results of the top thirty returned documents on a scale of one to five. Overall, material found on the two traditional services was ranked higher in relevance than that retrieved using Web search engines. Web information relevance ranged from the highest score of five, to the lowest score of one, while for the traditional services had a much smaller range, between three and five. However, information which was "either company-related or a popular current event was more likely to be up-to-date on the World Wide Web." The author noted that the quality of Web information is variable and unpredictable.

Chu and Rosenthal (1996) evaluated three search engines for response time and precision of search results. They used nine queries extracted from real reference questions at the Long Island University library, and one they composed to test the field search capability. Separate search queries were constructed for each search engine for their specific syntax. They found response time between the engines did not vary greatly. Relevance of retrieved records was determined by each of the authors separately. In calculating precision, the first ten records retrieved were evaluated. The average precision was calculated among all searches for every search engine in the study. AltaVista had the highest overall precision, followed by Lycos and Excite. Some queries were found not suitable for Web searching because of their complicated nature, pointing to the need to develop sophisticated facilities for search engines.

Tomaiuolo and Packer (1996) used two hundred search topics to assess five search engines. Both evaluative (provide ratings for Web sites) and non-evaluative engines were used in the study. The search topics included questions asked at Central Connecticut State University Library's reference information desk, topics from the *Reader's Guide to Periodicals*, and probable undergraduate topics. Attempts were made to optimize the query for each search engine by reading each engine's search tips, FAQs, and/or help documentation. Syntax affected the results due to the fact each engine is unique in the way it uses truncation, adjacency, etc., and many searches showed little evidence of overlap among the engines tested. Looking at only the first ten hits, the study found that the non-evaluative engines scored higher in both the number and relevancy of items retrieved with AltaVista and Infoseek generally performing well.

In 1995, Leighton began to use the criterion of precision to evaluate four Web index services. Two years later he conducted another study to correct the problems in his early project (Leighton & Srivastava, 1997; Leighton & Srivastava, 1999). Leighton and Srivastava examined five search engines using fifteen queries. Ten queries were obtained from the Winona State University Library reference desk and five from the Tomaiuolo study (every 20th question). In general, simple queries were used which did not take into account the advanced features of some search engines. The method used to judge "precision" was to evaluate the links on the Web documents. Five relevance categories were used: duplicate links, inactive links, irrelevant links, technically relevant links, potentially useful links, and the most probably useful links. The links were assigned weights from 0 (duplicate, inactive, and irrelevant) to 3 (most probably useful). The search engines were measured for their ability to put relevant pages within the first twenty links returned by a query. The results showed that the score one obtained greatly depend on how one defines relevant. If relevant is defined as the search being technically satisfied the overall precision was 0.81. If the definition of relevant is changed to only those links which are potentially useful the median precision drops to 0.39. If clearly useful is used the median is 0.06. Based on the precision of the first twenty URLs returned, AltaVista, Excite, and Infoseek did a significantly better job of delivering relevant documents.

As is true with most things connected with the Internet, changes in search engines are rapid as they continue to evolve. Given that fact, the above studies only allow some general conclusions to be drawn. As might be expected, traditional databases are more effective at finding relevant information, but the Internet is able to present more timely information especially related to current events (Feldman, 1998). Overall, the retrieval effectiveness of search engines is low, especially when looking at the studies where actual users were providing the relevance judgments. However, there are statistically significant differences in the effectiveness of various engines. For example, in several studies (Gordon & Pathak, 1999; Chu & Rosenthal, 1996; Leighton & Srivastava, 1999) AltaVista was one of the top ranked search engines compared to other engines being tested. It is important that students be made aware that many things affect an engine's effectiveness including: the capabilities it has in allowing a user to specify a search, the domain profile of its index, and the type of question being asked.

EVALUATION OF INTERNET INFORMATION

A major problem with Web based research is determining the quality of information retrieved. The Internet provides everyone with the opportunity to publish information. This means that a wide range of quality on virtually all subjects is available. There are generally no "gatekeepers" as there are for traditional print sources of information. As noted by Rettig (1996), many Internet sites that select and review resources rely on subjective values rather than focusing on information content. Originally Magellan's ratings for sites included timeliness and accuracy but it has dropped those criteria from its ratings, while it kept the criterion "net appeal" (Tomaiuolo & Packer, 1996). In a review of the criteria used by Internet evaluation sites, Smith (1997) found that appearance was one of the criteria used by the largest number of sites and that organization and ease of use along with currency were the criterion used second most often. In addition, students should be aware that some Internet search engines "sell" top space to advertisers who pay them to do so. This means that the sites listed first are not necessarily those which were ranked highest for relevance. *Caveat emptor* should be the mantra of students in the uncontrolled Internet environment. Rather than depending on evaluation sites or the ranking of search engines, students should be taught how to assess the quality of the information retrieved from the Web.

Katz (1997) considers content one of "the all-important evaluative points" in the assessment of reference sources, whether they are in print or electronic format. Many authors agree that the traditional criteria used to evaluate print reference sources are also appropriate for Web documents (Smith, 1997; Tate & Alexander, 1996). These criteria generally include accuracy, authority, objectivity, currency, and coverage. The traditional print criteria can be adopted for use in evaluating Web resources using some of the following methods.

Because many Web documents are not subject to the fact checks that are usually performed in traditional print resources the accuracy of the information presented should be assessed. The user should consider whether the page has passed through some type of review process. Some online journals use refereeing by editors or peers (Harris, 1997). A Web page that presents facts should clearly disclose the source of the information so the facts can be verified (Tate & Alexander, 1996). For research documents, the methodology used and the means of interpretation of data gathered and any statistical tests performed on it should be presented. A bibliography should be included for information provided from other sources. Information in the document can also be verified by comparison with print resources. Finally, the source of the information should be considered; for instance, company information obtained from the SEC's Edgar database may be more objective than a news release from the company itself.

Qualifications of the authors/editors and the reputations of the publishers are indicators of authoritative and credible content. "On a well-designed page, the organization responsible for publishing the information is made obvious and there is a clear statement of who the author is and what qualifies the author to write about the topic" (Tate & Alexander, 1996). The author's e-mail address should be provided. A search can be done on the author's name (using the full name in quotes) to try and identify the author's affiliation and qualifications. If possible, students should verify the identity of the server where the document is found. They should ask themselves the purpose of the organization publishing the document. Tillman (2000) considers the scope of the information included about authors/publishers and the ease of obtaining it as an indicator of quality.

Objectivity can start to be evaluated by looking for the stated purpose of the Web site and assessing its objectives. About one-fifth of the pages on the Internet are advertising (Wilkinson et al., 1997) where the main purpose is to generate sales rather than to inform. When on a company's Website one should assume the company is presenting facts in the most favorable light. For policy/political issues, one needs to assess the goals and objectives of the organization publishing the page. Additional things to consider include:

Are alternate points of view presented?

Is information presented out of context?

Most information is presented to support a point of view that the reader should take into account when reading and evaluating the page.

Timeliness or currency of information is also important. The Internet is particularly good at presenting up-to-date information related to companies and current events (Feldman, 1998). However, standard works on the Internet (Ex: Webster's Dictionary) are often old editions which are out-of-copyright and out-of-date (Rettig, 1995). Posting and copyright dates should be labeled, as well as the dates of any revisions to the page. The presence of outdated links indicate that a page is no longer being maintained and, therefore, the information presented may be out-of-date.

Coverage can be assessed by comparison to print resources which cover the same topic. Students need to assess whether the breadth and depth of the Web page is similar to the print source. One should also consider whether important facts, qualifications, consequences, or alternatives are presented. Users need to bear in mind whether a page can be properly viewed or if it requires special software. Additional considerations include whether there are options for text only, frames, or a suggested browser for better viewing.

As indicated in the points suggested under coverage, the unique nature of the Internet means criteria in addition to the standard ones for print resources, such as the quality of the links, navigation within the document, site access and usability, and software requirements, need to be considered (Tate & Alexander, 1996; Wilkinson et al., 1997). Several researchers at the University of Georgia identified 125 criteria as important in evaluating site and information quality on the Internet. These criteria were consolidated from 509 items named as possible evaluation measures by sources which included, but were not limited to, authorities on library reference materials and compilers of highly rated Internet resource lists. The criteria were arranged into eleven major categories. Four of the categories dealt primarily with the quality/usability of the site and contained 56 of the criteria and the remaining categories dealt primarily with the quality of the information on the site.

A set of panelists, consisting of 64 compilers of highly-ranked resource lists, were asked to rate each of the criteria two ways: (1) did the criteria apply to the site or experience using the site, the content within the site or both and (2) on a six point scale was the criteria 1, irrelevant, up to 6, essential. Responses were received from 49 of the panelists and the criteria were individually ranked both as indicators of information quality and of site quality. Only those criteria which were selected by at least 50% of the respondents as an indicator for either site or information quality were included in the individual lists for those items. The highest ranked indicators of site quality were (Oliver, 1998):

- Is there a good organizational scheme (e.g., by subject, format, audience, chronology, geography, authors, etc.)?
- Is the design so complex that it detracts from the content?
- Are readability and legibility guidelines followed (e.g., sufficient color and tone contrast between text and background, font size, doesn't use all caps, etc.)?
- Are the links clearly visible and understandable?

- Is there a consistent sense of context or understanding of position within the document at any given time?
- Does the use of graphics and icons contribute to the clarity and usability of the information?
- What is the URL of the document?

The highest ranked indicators of information quality were (Oliver, 1998):

- Is there a good organizational scheme (e.g., by subject, format, audience, chronology, geography, authors, etc.)?
- Is the information sufficiently current to meet the user's needs?
- Are there any obvious errors or misleading omissions in the document?
- Are the links relevant and appropriate to the document?
- What is the author's name?
- What is the author's professional or institutional affiliation?
- Does the author or the sponsor of the site have a vested or commercial interest in the topic?

It is interesting to note the highest ranked indicator of site quality was also the highest ranked indicator of information quality. This indicates there is significant overlap between these items, which makes it difficult to evaluate them separately. This is also true of the traditional criteria used in evaluating print resources. For example, the accuracy of facts presented is often related to the credibility of the author/publisher.

Many college library Websites have pages with links to popular search engines/directories and pages listing criteria to use in evaluating Internet information and tips on how that evaluation should be made. In addition to providing instruction on how to find and evaluate information on the Internet, Web based distance leaning programs should include links to the appropriate pages that provide this information at their institutions.

CONCLUSION

As technologies have continued to improve, the Internet has become a popular tool for presenting distance learning programs. In addition to being a means of delivery, the Internet provides learners with the ability to access information from a wide variety of sources. However, because the Internet is an unstructured environment, distances learners should have support in learning how to effectively use search engines to obtain required information and how to evaluate the information retrieved. This paper reviewed how search engines work, research comparing search engines, and evaluation criteria for information obtained on the Internet.

Research has shown that search engines index different pages so that an exhaustive search requires the use of several search engines. Research also shows that there are statistical differences in the performance of different search engines, with AltaVista ranking high in several studies. Nevertheless, different search engines appear to be better suited to different types of questions (Hsieh-Yee, 1998). Finally, the use of traditional evaluation criteria for print resources can be adopted for the evaluation of Internet information along with the use of additional criteria which are unique to the World Wide Web. By performing adequate evaluation of the information retrieved, distance-learning students can insure that the quality of the information they rely on is adequate for their purpose.

REFERENCES

Chu, H., & Rosenthal, M. (1996). Search Engines for the World Wide Web: A Comparative Study and Evaluation Methodology. *ASIS'96: Proceedings of the 59th ASIS Annual Meeting, 33*, 127-135.

Feldman, S. E. (1998). The Internet Search-Off: Results and Ruminations. In M. E. Williams (Ed.), *19th Annual National Online Meeting: Proceedings-1998.* Medford, NJ: Information Today, Inc.

Garman, N. (1999). Meta Search Engines. *Online, 23*(3), 74-78.

Gordon, M., & Pathak, P. (1999). Finding Information on the World Wide Web: the retrieval effectiveness of search engines. *Information Processing and Management, 35*(2), 141-180.

Harris, R. (1997). Evaluating Internet Research Sources. *[Online] Available: http://www.virtualsalt.com/evalu8it.htm*, (7/15/01).

Hill, M. (1998). Building a Support System for Distance Learning Students. *[Online] Available: http://www.coe.uh.edu/insite/elec_pub/HTML1998/de_hill.htm*, (6/5/01).

Hsieh-Yee, I. (1998). The Retrieval Power of Selected Search Engines: How Well Do They Address General Reference Questions and Subject Questions? *The Reference Librarian* (60), 24-27.

Johnson, W. T. (1999). Library Support for Distance Learning. *Community & Junior College Libraries, 8*(2), 51-57.

Lau, R. S. M. (2000). Issues and Outlook of E-Learning. *South Dakota Business Review, 59*(2), 1, 4.

Lawrence, S., & Giles, C. (1998). Searching the World Wide Web. *Science, 280*, 98-100.

Lehnert, W. G. (1998). *Internet101: a beginner's guide to the Internet and the WWW.* Reading, Massachusetts: Addison-Wesley.

Leighton, H. V., & Srivastava, J. (1997). Precision Among World Wide Web Search Services (Search Engines): Alta Vista, Excite, Hotbot, Infoseek, Lycos. *Available: http://www.winona.msus.edu/library/webind2/webind2.htm*, (4/15/99).

Leighton, H. V., & Srivastava, J. (1999). First 20 Precision among World Wide Web Search Services (Search Engines). *Journal of the American Society for Information Science, 50*(10), 870-881.

Liu, J. (1996). Understanding WWW Search Tools. *Available: http://www.indiana. edu/~librcsd/search/*, (11/24/97).

Liu, J. (1998). Guide to Meta-Search Engines. *Business & Finance Bulletin* (107), 17-20.

Martinez, A. M., & Sanchez, E. F. (1999). Comparing Internet Search Tools. *Proceeding of the International Online Information Meeting* (December 7, 1999), 263-266.

O'Leary, M. (2000). Distance Learning and Libraries. *Online, 24*(4), 94-96.

Oliver, K. M. (1998). *Evaluation Procedures for WWW Information Resources: A Final Project Report.* Paper presented at the annual convention of the Association For Educational Communications and Technology (AECT), St. Louis, Mo.

Oliver, K. M., Wilkinson, G. L., & Bennett, L. T. (1997). Evaluating the Quality of Internet Information Sources. *[Online] Available: http://www.edtech.vt.edu/edtech/ kmoliver/webeval/AACE97.html*, (7/13/01).

Rettig, J. (1995). Putting the Squeeze on the Information Firehose: The Need for 'Neteditors and 'Netreviewers. *[Online] Available: http://www.swem.wm.edu/ firehose.html*, (7/13/01).

Rettig, J. (1996). Beyond "Cool" Analog Models for Reviewing Digital Resources. *Online, 20*(5), 52-64.

Smith, A. G. (1997). Testing the Surf: Criteria for Evaluating Internet Information Resources. *[Online] Available: http://info.lib.uh.edu/pr/v8/n3/smit8n3.html*, (7/13/01).

Sullivan, D. (1999a). Crawling Under the Hood: An Update on Search Engine Technology. *Online, 23*(3), 30-38.

Sullivan, D. (1999b). Search Engine Report. *Search Engine Watch, 2 Nov. 1999, [Online] Available: http://searchenginewatch.com*, (11/3/99).

Tate, M., & Alexander, J. (1996). Teaching Critical Evaluation Skills for World Wide Web Resources. *Computers in Libraries, 16*, 49-55.

Tillman, H. N. (2000). Evaluating Quality on the Net. *[Online] Available: http:// www.hopetillman.com/findqual.html*, (7/13/01).

Tomaiuolo, N. G., & Packer, J. G. (1996). An Analysis of Internet Search Engines: Assessment of Over 200 Search Queries. *Computers in Libraries, 16*, 58-62.

Wilkinson, G. L., Bennett, L. T., & Oliver, K. M. (1997). Evaluation Criteria and Indicators of Quality for Internet Resources. *Educational Technology, 37*(3), 52-59.

Yahoo! Do You Google?
Virtual Reference Overview

Nancy Cannon

SUMMARY. The Internet is fast becoming the world's largest public library. Reference librarians are using Web resources rather than print to answer many reference queries. This article provides an overview of topics relating to virtual reference services: search engines, subject directories, virtual reference desks, the invisible Web, electronic journal publishing, virtual reference services, and reference librarian skills. *[Article copies available for a fee from The Haworth Document Delivery Service: 1-800-HAWORTH. E-mail address: <getinfo@haworthpressinc.com> Website: <http://www.HaworthPress.com> © 2002 by The Haworth Press, Inc. All rights reserved.]*

KEYWORDS. Distance learning, virtual reference services, search engines, online journals

INTRODUCTION

In 1945 Vannevar Bush imagined a desk-sized machine he called a "memex," which could store books, records, and communications and would be mecha-

Nancy Cannon is Electronic Resources Coordinator/Reference Librarian, Milne Library, SUNY Oneonta, Oneonta, NY 13820 (E-mail: cannonns@snyoneva.cc.oneonta. edu).

"Googling is using the popular search engine Google.com to look up someone's name in an effort to find out more about them. You might Google your neighbor, your old college roommate, or someone you've recently met to see what information is available about them on the Internet" ("Googling").

[Haworth co-indexing entry note]: "Yahoo! Do You Google? Virtual Reference Overview." Cannon, Nancy. Co-published simultaneously in *The Reference Librarian* (The Haworth Information Press, an imprint of The Haworth Press, Inc.) No. 77, 2002, pp. 31-37; and: *Distance Learning: Information Access and Services for Virtual Users* (ed: Hemalata Iyer) The Haworth Information Press, an imprint of The Haworth Press, Inc., 2002, pp. 31-37. Single or multiple copies of this article are available for a fee from The Haworth Document Delivery Service [1-800-HAWORTH, 9:00 a.m. - 5:00 p.m. (EST). E-mail address: getinfo@ haworthpressinc.com].

nized so it could be consulted with great speed and flexibility. An essential feature of the memex was the idea of associative indexing, "whereby any item may be caused at will to select immediately and automatically another" (Bush, 107). This is very similar to the concept of hypertext, developed by Tim Berners-Lee while he was a researcher at Conseil Européenne pour la Recherche Nucleaire (CERN). In 1993, Marc Andreesen led a team that developed *Mosaic*, a graphic interface browser that allowed users to point and click to navigate the Web. Later, Andreesen worked on the development of *Netscape* (Gribble). The impact of this technology on library reference services (and the world) has been immense. The Internet is becoming the world's largest public library as well as the library of first choice for many users. This article provides an overview of topics relating to virtual reference services: search engines, subject directories, virtual reference desks, the invisible Web, electronic journal publishing, reference librarian skills, and virtual reference services.

SEARCH ENGINES

Search engines are the first (and last) tools many people use to find information on the Web. In order to effectively use search engines, it is necessary to know how they work. Despite popular belief, search engines do not scan the Web as a search is entered and look for a match. Software robots, called "spiders," first build lists of words found on Web sites. An index is kept of words and where they can be found. Users of search engines look for words in the index of that search engine. Since building the index can be very time consuming (and expensive), search engines do not necessarily update their index very often. This is why a link to a page on a search engine results list may retrieve an error message such as "Error 404–File Not Found." The results can be further skewed by commercial enterprises that pay to have their pages listed in a prominent location. Therefore, a search on "geriatric medicine" may list pages that are ads for *Viagra* before Web sites such as the *National Institutes of Health*. A recent trend is for some search and directory firms to ask for money from sites that want to be included in their listings (Plotkin). These search services may miss worthwhile government and educational as well as some commercial sites. Fortunately for end-users, software developers are continually competing to develop the best search engines. For example, *Google (http:// www.google.com/)* increased the relevancy of searches by using link popularity as a criterion for the order of listing: the more hits and links a page receives, the higher it is on the results list. "The heart of *Google*'s search technology is PigeonRank™, a system for ranking Web pages developed by *Google* founder Larry Page and Sergey Brin at Stanford University. Building upon the breakthrough work of B. F. Skinner, Page and Brin reasoned that low cost pigeon clusters (PCs) could be used to compute the relative value of Web pages faster than human editors or machine-based algorithms" ("Technology Behind *Google*'s Great Results"). *Vivisimo (http://vivisimo.com),* winner of the 2001 *Search Engine Watch* award *(http://searchenginewatch.com/awards/2001-winners.html)* for metasearch engines, is a new generation metasearch engine. Listings are clustered into topics so the user can quickly navigate the results. Quantity of hits does not seem to be a problem with any of the search engines. Results are sometimes poor due to paid placements, irrelevant hits, worthless content, or an overwhelming number of hits. Future advances in search engines will likely concentrate on improving the speed and relevancy of results. Keeping abreast of new and improved search tools is a challenge for reference librarians. There are many Web sites that rate search engines. Two good ones are *Search Engine Watch (http://searchenginewatch.com)* and *SearchIQ (http.//www.zdnet.com/searchiq/directory/multi.html).*

SUBJECT DIRECTORIES

Unlike a search engine that relies on software to find results, humans select and organize the listings in a subject directory. Directories can be a good way to find the "best" sites on topic. Some search engines (such as *Yahoo*) are a combination of a subject directory and a search engine. One very useful directory is the *Open Directory Project (http://dmoz.org/),* which has over 3,000,000 URLs and 46,000 volunteer editors. The *Open Directory Project,* founded in the spirit of the Open Source movement, is used as a core directory by search engines and portals such as *Google, Netscape Search, Lycos, AOL Search,* and *HotBot.* There are many good librarian created directories that can be used to answer reference queries. For example, the *Librarians Index to the Internet (http://lii.org/),* a searchable, annotated subject directory of more than 9,000 Internet resources, is funded by the Library of California and the Institute of Museum and Library Services. In addition to several paid staff members, more than 100 librarians work as volunteer indexers. There are stringent selection criteria for inclusion including content, authority, scope, and design. *LII* is an excellent resource for general reference questions. For scholarly Internet resource collections, *Infomine (http://infomine.ucr.edu/),* with over 23,000 librarian-selected sites, is a good place to search. *Infomine,* developed and supported by the Library of the University of California, Riverside, is a federally funded project which utilizes the services of librarian volunteers. It is arranged by subject and is searchable as well. There are several helpful free e-mail services reference librarians can use to keep current, including those offered by *The Internet Scout Report (http://scout.cs.wisc.edu/), Librarians' Index to the Internet (http://lii.org/),* and *Virtual Acquisition Shelf & News (http://resourceshelfblogspot.com).*

VIRTUAL REFERENCE DESKS

Another form of subject directory is a virtual reference desk created by an individual library primarily to meet the reference needs of their clientele. In addition to free sites, library-created sites usually include subscription databases. Although some reference sources, such as statistics books, are currently easier to use in print than electronic format, library users often prefer an electronic version. It is likely that the number of classic reference works available in electronic format will increase and many print sources will gradually fade away. With the wealth of Internet reference sources available, the creation and maintenance of a library-created virtual reference desk can seem overwhelming, especially for a library with a small staff. Some libraries find it more efficient to simply link to virtual reference desks at other institutions rather than creating their own. Libraries with subscription reference databases or wishing to target information to their own unique audience will serve their users better by creating their own. Library administrators need to set priorities so library-created Web pages are kept current. Since activity at physical reference desks is declining, offering targeted reference sources though a library-created virtual reference desk can be one good way to reach cyberpatrons.

THE INVISIBLE WEB

The "invisible Web" is another resource for virtual reference materials. The invisible Web, thought to be 500 times larger than the visible Web, is that part of the Web that is not searched by standard search engines. Most of the invisible Web is made up of the contents of thousands of databases that can be searched individually but are not reachable by standard search engines. In addition, the invisible Web includes non-indexed pages such as images, fee-based services, pages that require registration, and sites behind firewalls. Library subscription databases and OPACs are part of the invisible Web. Other examples include phone books, dictionaries, electronic books and journals, encyclopedias, digital libraries, financial databases, and term paper mills. There are several ways to find invisible Web databases. One way is to use a standard search engine such as *Google* and do a search on the topic and the word "database," e.g., *language database*. Web sites have been created specifically to enable the user to find this hidden information, e.g., *www.invisibleweb.com*.

For academic use, *Librarians Index to the Internet (http://lii.org/)*, *AcademicInfo (http://www.academicinfo.net/index.html)*, and *Infomine (http://infomine.ucr.edu/)* are good choices. *Queryserver (http://www.queryserver.com/)*, a metasearch engine, allows the user to search either a user-selected group of standard search engines or Web sites and databases listed by topic.

This combination approach by topic is easy to use and will probably emerge in an even more sophisticated form in the future.

JOURNAL ARTICLES

The availability to researchers of journal articles is greatly influenced by trends in the publishing industry. One typical model of publishing academic papers is likely to change. Under this system, college professors submit papers to publishers and receive no monetary compensation. In addition, the author often signs over the copyright to the publisher who prints and distributes the journal in either print or electronic format or both. College libraries then purchase subscriptions to the journals with articles written by the college professors, often at very great costs. The cost of journal subscriptions has far exceeded the rate of inflation, causing the libraries to be forced to cut journal titles. This in turn forces the publishers to raise prices. "What keeps the publishers' situation from being hopeless is the tremendous inertia of the scholarly community, which impedes the transition to free or inexpensive electronic journals. Another factor in the publishers' favor is that there are other unnecessary costs that can be squeezed, namely those of the libraries. Moreover, the unnecessary library costs are far greater than those of publishers, which creates an opportunity for the latter to exploit and thereby to retain their position" (Odlyzko). A different model is that used by the e-print *arXiv (xxx.arXiv.cornell. edu)*, a physics preprint service supported by the National Science Foundation and Cornell University. Papers are submitted full-text by the author directly to the database. There is no peer-review process. The cost of this distribution method is significantly less than the usual scholar/publisher/library route (Ginsparg). The eScholarship program from the *California Digital Library (http://escholarship.cdlib.org/?main=2)* is an example of a group that is experimenting with alternative means of producing and disseminating scholarly materials. It is likely that the availability of scholarly information to users without large pocketbooks will increase as a result of these endeavors.

VIRTUAL REFERENCE SERVICES

Many libraries provide some type of virtual reference service. E-mail question/answer services are one simple and effective method. Some libraries use software such as *AOL Instant Messenger* to provide a real-time experience. Chat software has been tried with varying degrees of success. Providing virtual reference service 24/7 is now the goal for some libraries. For example, the Library of Congress created the *Collaborative Digital Reference Service (CDRS)* a "library to library" network for asking and answering reference questions *(http://www.loc.gov/rr/digiref/)*. Libraries from all over the world have volunteered to participate in the project. In addition to the Internet, the *CDRS* is designed to utilize the millions of print and electronic resources held by libraries that are not online. Participating libraries are thus able to expand the reference services they offer end users. Similarly, there are several Web-based question/answer services that use qualified volunteers to answer questions. *AllExperts (http://allexperts.com/)* is a free service that uses thousands of volunteer experts (such as carpenters, physicians, biologists, plumbers, auto mechanics, gardeners, engineers) to answer questions. Never has the opportunity to ask an expert a question been so great.

REFERENCE LIBRARIAN SKILLS

Reference librarians who navigate the uncharted waters of providing virtual reference services need to develop certain skills if they are not to be swept away by change. Perhaps foremost is the need to continually research new searching methods and Web sources for scholarly content. Print materials cannot be forgotten. In this new world, computer literacy, flexibility, and the ability to respond quickly and accurately can be more useful than an out of date second master's degree. Reference librarians need to adapt to different ways of conducting the reference interview, maintaining contact with the user, and composing answers to someone who is not in the physical library. New methods of delivering information must continually be investigated. Librarians can't just be in sync with virtual users, but must strive to stay ahead of them.

THE FUTURE

What is the future of virtual libraries? Vannevar Bush commented in 1945, "The difficulty seems to be, not so much that we publish unduly in view of the extent and variety of present day interests, but rather that publication has been extended far beyond our present ability to make real use of the record. The summation of human experience is being expanded at a prodigious rate, and the means we use for threading through the consequent maze to the momentarily important item is the same as was used in the days of square-rigged ships" (Bush, 102). In 50 years we have moved far beyond the days of square-rigged ships to personal computers, hypertext, and the Internet. Hundreds of thousands of worldwide contributors, including libraries, universities, governments, organizations, commercial enterprises, and individuals have created an immense virtual library that continues to expand. Yet, the means we use for "threading through the consequent maze" still sometimes falls short. "Imagination is more important than knowledge. Knowledge is limited. Imagination encircles the world" (Albert Einstein).

REFERENCES

Bush, Vannevar. "As We May Think." *Atlantic Monthly* July 1945: 101-108.

Ginsparg, Paul. "Creating a global knowledge network" 20 Feb. 2001. Second Joint ICSU Press-UNESCO Expert Conference on Electronic Publishing in Science. 14 March 2002. <http://arxiv.org/blurb/pg01unesco.html>.

"Googling." 9 March 2002. SearchWebManagement. 25 March 2002. <http://search WebManagement.techtarget.com/sDefinition/0,,sid27_gci799367,00.html>.

Gribble, Cheryl. "History of the Web Beginning at CERN." *Hitmill*. 20 Oct. 2001. 28 March 2002. <http://www.hitmill.com/internet/web_history.html>.

Odlyzko, Andrew. "Competition and Cooperation: Libraries and Publishers in the Transition to Electronic Scholarly Journals." *Journal of Electronic Publishing* 4:4 (June, 1999). <http://www.press.umich.edu/jep/04-04/odlyzko0404.html>.

Plotkin, Hal. "Search Me: Doom Ahead for Search Engines that Charge Fees." *Tech Beat*. 28 Jan. 2002. SF Gate. 27 March 2002. <http://www.sfgate.com/cgi-bin/article. cgi?file=/gate/archive/2002/01/28/srcheng.DTL>.

"Technology Behind Google's Great Results." 2002. Our Search: Google Technology. 14 March 2002. <http://www.google.com/technology/pigeonrank.html>.

The Growing
and Changing Role of Consortia
in Providing Direct and Indirect Support
for Distance Higher Education

Jane M. Subramanian

SUMMARY. Consortia and cooperative efforts in the library world have had a long history, and their importance has been recognized even from the start. As the twentieth century has progressed, consortia have become even more important, and the extent of their roles has broadened considerably. In the last few years, they have become large players in helping libraries build shared online catalogs and assisting libraries in affording purchases of electronic resources, both important elements of support for distance learners. As the number of distance learners increases at colleges and universities throughout the country, consortia will be increasingly important to library support of distance learners in their information needs. *[Article copies available for a fee from The Haworth Document Delivery Service: 1-800-HAWORTH. E-mail address: <getinfo@ haworthpressinc.com> Website: <http://www.HaworthPress.com> © 2002 by The Haworth Press, Inc. All rights reserved.]*

KEYWORDS. Distance learning, consortia, electronic resources, virtual reference services

Jane M. Subramanian is Archivist/Music Cataloger/Reference Librarian, F. W. Crumb Memorial Library, SUNY Potsdam, Potsdam, NY 13676 (E-mail: subramjm@ potsdam.edu).

[Haworth co-indexing entry note]: "The Growing and Changing Role of Consortia in Providing Direct and Indirect Support for Distance Higher Education." Subramanian, Jane M. Co-published simultaneously in *The Reference Librarian* (The Haworth Information Press, an imprint of The Haworth Press, Inc.) No. 77, 2002, pp. 39-62; and: *Distance Learning: Information Access and Services for Virtual Users* (ed: Hemalata Iyer) The Haworth Information Press, an imprint of The Haworth Press, Inc., 2002, pp. 39-62. Single or multiple copies of this article are available for a fee from The Haworth Document Delivery Service [1-800-HAWORTH, 9:00 a.m. - 5:00 p.m. (EST). E-mail address: getinfo@haworthpressinc.com].

INTRODUCTION

The existence of consortia is frequently viewed as a more recent development in the 20th century, but in fact, cooperation and consortia in the library realm have been with us for quite some time. The long tradition of library cooperative efforts actually began in the last quarter of the 1800s, when the American Library Association created a Committee on Cooperation in Indexing and Cataloguing in 1876, one of the first appearances of library cooperation. The idea of shared cataloging thus had early roots, with the American Library Association beginning to publish their analytic cards in the 1890s (Alexander, 1999). Even interlibrary loan first emerged around the same time and assumed a very important role from the start. Some of the first signs of interlibrary loan included evidence of the librarian of the University of California announcing in 1898 that "he would be willing to lend books from his library to those that would reciprocate" and at Princeton a year later, the librarian there proposed "a lending library for libraries" (Alexander, 1999).

The earliest known article on the subject appeared in 1879 with G. L. Campbell's "Grouping of Places for Library Purposes" (Kopp, 1998). Melville Dewey himself spoke about cooperative efforts in 1886 with his writing on "Library Co-operation" in an issue of *Library Journal*, with E. A. Mac a year earlier publishing an article titled "Co-operation Versus Competition" (Kopp, 1998). In 1905, an article was written in *Public Libraries* titled "Universal Library: A Plea for Placing Any Desired Book within the Reach of Any Person Wishing to Make Reasonable Use of Same" (Kopp, 1998). Clearly, the desire to expand resources beyond that available at the closest location had early roots, along with group efforts to accomplish this task as well.

One of the first of the strictly academic library consortia was a group called Triangle Research Libraries Network, which formed in 1933 as related to the Committee on Intellectual Cooperation first initiated by University of North Carolina and Duke (Bostick, 2001). It is clear from early evidence that cooperation has always been important for libraries, but a major study in the 1970s of academic consortia by the U.S. Office of Education (Kopp, 1998) emphasizes the view of their importance at that point in the century as well.

The 1970s and 1980s saw the continued growth of consortia, but other activities became significant at that time, such as the advent of bibliographic utilities, or as Kopp terms them, "megaconsortia," as well as the rise of local integrated library systems. He goes on to comment: "Although both of these factors would also enhance involvement in library consortia, they seemed to draw attention away from consortial activity during the period when libraries were concentrating on getting one or both of these technological endeavors up and running" (Kopp, 1998).

EARLY ROLES OF CONSORTIA
AND GROWTH OF TYPES OF CONSORTIA

Early consortial roles included the Library of Congress's distribution of catalog cards to participating libraries (Bostick, 2001) and as mentioned earlier, the sharing of resources, including of course the all-important role of interlibrary loan. The role of consortia expanded to include library automation initiatives in the '60s and '70s, which was also the period of rapid growth of consortia throughout the country (Bostick, 2001).

Joint purchase endeavors and reciprocal access agreements also began to develop. All of these group efforts involved attempts to expand availability of library resources to students and faculty and to increase the buying power of limited library budgets. Reciprocal access was another means of increasing the available resources to patrons within a close geographic area, allowing libraries with limited space and finances to expand availability of library resources for their patrons. In our own geographic area, the Associated Colleges consortium, a group that includes Clarkson University, SUNY Canton, St. Lawrence University, and SUNY Potsdam, our own campus, developed a relationship that included reciprocal borrowing privileges, and in addition, our students have an added benefit of reciprocal borrowing privileges within the large SUNY system. Joint purchase of print resources to be shared, such as collection development grants and other funding opportunities, further enhanced the collections of member libraries.

Many consortial efforts also made strong progress in increasing efficiency and expanding access through such bibliographic utilities as OCLC, RILN, and other kinds of union catalogs for identifying locations of materials, etc. As staffing cutbacks hit many libraries in the last part of the century, these utilities helped libraries cope by providing shared cataloging. This allowed libraries to try to continue to provide quality services, although most times with a price tag attached.

As the pace and quantity of information resources increased, the role of interlibrary loan escalated rapidly. The importance of scholarly research at institutions of higher education increased the need for access to all material available on a given subject. The trend toward specialization within disciplines also escalated the need for more material on a specific topic than could be housed in most libraries.

During these time periods, the idea of distance education mainly consisted of correspondence courses by mail, where the types of coursework placed less emphasis on the need for library resources, and the student used whatever library was located nearby geographically if they did need to use a library. There was little need, therefore, for library support from the institution offering the courses.

Throughout the twentieth century, the types of consortia have been chang-ing and expanding. Local consortia seemed the most popular in type initially, but over the years, statewide consortia became increasingly important and prevalent, with national types and consortia by similar type of library increas-ing as well. The expansion of the number of state consortia is well represented in the literature, and the statewide thrusts are too numerous to even begin to mention here. Some examples, however, include MELVYL in California (Saunders, 1999), CARL in Colorado (Saunders, 1999), ILCSO (Illinois Li-brary Computer Systems Organization) (Sloan, 1998), GALILEO (Georgia Library Learning Online) (Potter, 1997), Louisiana Library Network (Potter, 1997), OHIOLINK (Thornton, 2000), TEXSHARE (Potter, 1997), VIVA (Virtual Library of Virginia) (Potter, 1997), PORTALS (Portland Area Li-brary System) in the Portland, Oregon and Vancouver area (Rohe, 2000), WRLC (Washington Research Library Consortium) in Maryland and Wash-ington, D.C. (Payne, 1998), UTAD (Utah Article Delivery Service) in Utah (Kochan, 1998), and the SUNYConnect thrust in New York. The purposes and services for each of these statewide consortia vary from one to another, with some limiting their scope to just one or a few initiatives while others such as the WRLC, which shares book collections, an online union catalog, electronic resources collections, offsite storage facility, and separately staffed service (Payne, 1998). Some, such as three SUNY university campuses (Buffalo, Binghamton, and Stony Brook) and CUNY, created an alliance to share elec-tronic indexes, in this case via NOTIS Systems PACLink software, along with a delivery system called SUNY Express (Rogers, 1994). As indicated by Pot-ter, "Virtually every state has some level of formal resource sharing among its academic libraries with Illinois, Minnesota, Wisconsin, Ohio, California, and Missouri being among the most advanced in their efforts over the past two de-cades" (Potter, 1997).

Potter also points out that "for most academic libraries, statewide coopera-tion offers distinct advantages and incentives" (Potter, 1997). He goes on to note that political and geographical grouping is involved, and these libraries "often share common social and cultural bodies," as well as "pride of place." Even interlibrary loan shows much higher interaction within states, as one study done in Illinois has shown (Wiley, 2000). Given the usual quicker deliv-ery time within a closer geographic area, this makes sense. The greater trend in consortia toward statewide efforts is especially helpful for distance learners because there is more apt to be a participating library available closer to them geographically if needs arise for them to physically use a library. Direct mail delivery to distance learners is also usually faster within a closer geographic area.

There are a growing number of consortia by similar type of library. One ex-ample is the Center for Research Libraries (CRL), which consists of college, university, and other scholarly collections in North America. The cooperative collection development programme and joint building for housing of less frequently used material opens up larger collections of rarely held primary research materials to researchers of its members, which include the major research libraries. The elements of the Global Newspapers Component, Current Serials Component, Retrospective Collections Component, Foreign Doctoral Dissertations Component, and Area Studies Component provide a wealth of material that would not otherwise be available (Simpson, 1998).

The existence of consortia is also increasing in other ways at the national level. The Network Alliance, just one example, includes 16 networks spanning most of North America and their goal is to help libraries and publishers find cost-effective licensing opportunities (Baker, 2000). In addition to library consortia, other national consortia are very important for the future. One example is the World Wide Web Consortium. This group's focus on "common protocols and interoperability, is important to the continued evolution of the Web as a platform for resource sharing" (Balas, 1998). More extensive possibilities exist in the future, such as Alan Charnes' view of the consortial structure as ultimately the way to achieve a National Electronic Library (Kopp, 1998).

Consortia are well under way in other countries as well, although some nations have political and social characteristics that lend them more easily to cooperative efforts than others. As Kyrillidou comments, "the European consortia find themselves in a linguistically and culturally diverse and dispersed environment. Central government control is one way to bring some unity and a sense of common direction" (Kyrillidou, 1999). This problem, however, can also be looked at in a positive fashion as well, in that the linguistic and cultural differences will eventually provide a tremendously rich diversity of material and outlook. Hopefully the further linking of the United States with some of these richly diverse collections will help to expand our patrons' access to a greater breadth of material.

There are numerous consortia that have a presence in other countries. Just a few examples include: CURL (Consortium of University Research Libraries) in the United Kingdom (Carr, 1998); LAMDA (London and Manchester Document Access) electronic document delivery in the UK (Williams, 1997); CAUL in Australia, similar to the Association of Research Libraries (Kyrillidou, 1999); UKB, a Dutch consortium; GBV in Germany (Kyrillidou, 1999); several different networks such as NISSAT, HELLIS, INFLIBNET, and VIDYANET, and ERNET in India and Asia (Gayas-ud-din, 1993); SBN network, territorial library systems, and sectoral cooperation in Italy (Giordano, 2000); InfoSpring Digital Library Project in Taiwan (Ke, 2000); Elsevier ScienceDirect OnSite China Consortium in conjunction with Tsinghua University in Beijing and Shanghai Jiaotong University in Shanghai, China (ScienceDirect, 2000); ULAKBIM in Turkey (Tonta, 2001); Couperin in France (Reibel, 2000), and many others, as discussed in the published proceedings of an International Conference in Italy in 1999 (Connolly, 2000).

In addition, there is now a new international thrust with the advent of the International Coalition of Library Consortia (ICOLC), first started as a loosely structured group named Consortium of Consortia in the mid-1990s (Bostick, 2001). This important group has begun groundbreaking work to provide a framework for consortial efforts worldwide. In their recently released statement on selection and purchase of electronic information, they indicate their "primary intention is to define the current conditions and preferred practices for pricing and delivering scholarly information within this emerging electronic environment" (International Coalition of Library Consortia, 1998). Other international thrusts exist as well, such as SPARC (Scholarly Publishing and Academic Resources Coalition), whose main goal has been to influence a lower cost of scholarly information (Michalak, 2000) and whose accomplishments already include BioOne, a fulltext database in the sciences and a partnership effort of five organizations (SPARC, 1999). Another example of an international consortia is one that started out as a statewide group, Library Services Alliance of New Mexico, and later expanded into an international organization of 13 members, consisting of a partnership involving both academic and government research libraries (Curtis, 2000). Kyrillidou sees an increase in cooperation at the international level that "may lead to formal international cooperation to foster global access" (Kyrillidou, 1999).

With national and international consortia, eventually we should be able to develop closer links both at home and abroad. Hopefully, stronger and broader consortial efforts will eventually result in access to many more resources of wider scope. This will be an invaluable addition to all of our students, but especially for distance students, who will begin to have access to a broader range of resources than at present.

CONSORTIA EXPANDING INTO NEW ROLES: IMPACT FOR DISTANCE LEARNERS

As we enter the 21st century, the role of consortia has become of ultimate importance as distance education has appeared full force on the horizon. The college student profile increasingly includes higher numbers of non-traditional students, and students' lives include not only working either part-time or full-time, but sometimes other family caretaking duties as well, leaving less time for the truly dedicated student to spend time physically on campus. The availability of e-mail and even more immediate Internet contact such as instant messenger have also allowed students to stay in much closer contact with their faculty instructors, even from a distance, as well as librarians and the library. Computer technology, telephone and video conferencing all allow people to carry on discussions from a distance, as well as "attend" meetings or classes while remaining geographically separated by hundreds of miles or more. These same technologies have become increasingly important for libraries in providing services to a wider array of patrons.

The Association of College and Research Libraries has issued revised *Guidelines for Distance Learning Library Services*, approved by the ALA Standards Committee in fall 2000. The guidelines define distance learning library services as "those library services in support of college, university, or other post-secondary courses and programs offered away from a main campus, or in the absence of a traditional campus, and regardless of where credit is given. These courses may be taught in traditional or non-traditional formats or media, may or may not require physical facilities, and may or may not involve live interactions of teachers and students." The guidelines also include the important statement, "Access to adequate library services and resources is essential for the attainment of superior academic skills in post-secondary education, regardless of where students, faculty, and programs are located. Members of the distance learning community are entitled to library services resources equivalent to those provided for students and faculty in traditional campus settings" (Association of College and Research Libraries, 2000). The guidelines go on to list the following services as essential: (1) reference assistance; (2) computer-based bibliographic and informational services; (3) reliable, rapid, secure access to institutional and other networks including the Internet; (4) consultation services; (5) a program of library user instruction designed to instill independent and effective information literacy skills while specifically meeting the learner-support needs of the distance learning community; (6) assistance with and instruction in the use of nonprint media and equipment; (7) reciprocal or contractual borrowing, or interlibrary loan services using broadest application of fair use of copyrighted materials; (8) prompt document delivery such as a courier system and/or electronic transmission; (9) access to reserve materials in accordance with copyright fair use policies; (10) adequate service hours for optimum access by users; and (11) promotion of library services to the distance learning community, including documented and updated policies, regulations, and procedures for systematic development, and management of information resources.

The technological age has been a real boon, but has also created the necessity for students to learn in a different manner at times, and for faculty and students to interact differently. The whole idea of distributed education, a newer terminology in use as a broader concept than distance education, focuses on a whole range of interactive learning between student and professor, not confined to time and place. A recent publication of EDUCAUSE and the American Council on Education describes distributed learning as learning that "can occur either on or off campus, providing students with greater flexibility and eliminating time as a barrier to learning . . . Distributed learning extends the opportunities for interaction between faculty and student, incorporating simulations and visualizations, as well as collaborative learning" (Oblinger, 2001). This publication also discusses how students learn differently today, an important aspect to remember in terms of providing library services to distance learners. The importance of partnerships and sharing of resources is also emphasized. However, the statement is also made that "Perhaps the greatest obstacle to creating a complex and comprehensive set of distributed learning offerings lies in meeting the information needs of students in an electronic medium" (Oblinger, 2001). Although in-person verbal communication is still very important, more and more of those in higher education must learn to communicate from a distance, without the benefit of the important facial and gesture cues. Part of the difficult task included in the new environment is for librarians and information specialists to find ways to adequately provide assistance for distance learners in their information needs, including the provision of adequate information resources for their course needs and how best to interact with patrons in a technological environment.

The role of consortia has also changed a great deal over the past few years. Barbara Allen and Arnold Hirshon's article begins with an appropriate quote from Benjamin Franklin, "We must all hang together, or assuredly we shall all hang separately" (Allen, 1998). They then go on to comment, "Perhaps the important development for academic libraries during the current decade has been the move from organizational self-sufficiency to a collaborative survival mode as personified by the growth of library consortia. Information technology is now enabling a level of cooperation that is much broader and deeper than ever before. Since about 1990, changes in technology such as virtual union catalogs and the growth of the World Wide Web have substantially changed the ways in which libraries share collections, and work to share resources " (Allen, 1998).

Given that most library budgets have not increased much in the last few years, rarely keeping up with inflation if they have risen at all, the costs of purchasing expensive electronic resources to help provide for the needs of students on and off campus can seem daunting. As colleges and universities add distance programs, there frequently is little or no increase in library support to provide resources and assistance for students enrolled in distance classes. The availability of consortial help in support of libraries in their efforts to develop the means to support these students has been a godsend.

Many types of consortia have previously provided shared resources in terms of print and other types of formats, but with the explosion of the availability of electronic resources with their high price tags, the thrusts involving the joint purchase of materials by consortia have become increasingly important. Negotiated group purchases many times result in significant price reductions for each participant, sometimes allowing the purchase of some electronic material that might otherwise not be possible, especially for smaller institutions with more limited budgets. Although restrictions may apply in the use of the materials, the gains made excel over the limitations. However, Bostick points out that "few consortia are just 'buying clubs' anymore" (Bostick, 2001), thus, although joint purchase opportunities is one role of consortia, it is only one aspect of important consortia activities.

Consortia have also become involved in joint purchases of other types of electronic resources beyond fulltext periodicals. For example, here in the SUNY system, a collection of eBooks from netLibrary was purchased for all SUNY campuses. Another area of electronic sharing is digitization of rare book and archival collections, such as VIVA's explorations (Potter, 1997). Faculty, students, and other researchers have been "distance students" in terms of physical access to these types of collections even in the past. Other different kinds of efforts include BYTES, Books You Teach Every Semester, which is a project to examine "information about reserve collections in history and literature in the English language at eight of the eighteen NERL participating university libraries and attempting to answer underlying questions about how best to digitize critical resources for teaching these subjects" (Landesman, 2000). Another example is VIVA's exploration of "how it might influence teaching-learning models" (Potter, 1997) and their work on a different type of project, funded by a NEH grant, for creating a time line of Virginia history (Oder, 2000). The latter is clearly the type of project that is beneficial for not just all academic libraries in the state, but for school and public libraries as well.

Further expansion of joint automated systems has also increased in recent years. In some instances, joint automated systems have been possible at the statewide consortia level, such as California's MELVYL system, and SUNY's new thrust, SUNYConnect in New York State. Many institutions would have difficulty affording online systems if they had to come up with the full purchase price alone, and consortia have begun to play an important role here as well. In addition to providing affordability for purchasing a system, other benefits of joint systems are significant as well, including patron access to a larger collection of holdings. Arranging and assisting with training of the institutions involved is also a strong benefit. One group paving the way for other institutions in the consortia by providing information, tips, and solutions for the rest, so that each library doesn't have to re-invent the wheel on its own, especially if constrained by limited staffing, is an ultimate benefit. As pilot sites experiment and learn the ropes, they can provide invaluable help to the rest. In the SUNY system, librarians from one or more SUNY libraries are sometimes hired on a part-time negotiated release situation from their own campus, or on full-time leave, to assist in the project of helping to bring other SUNY libraries up in their systems.

While electronic resources allow much access to information resources from a distance, there are many significant materials that are available only in print at present, and most will remain that way for the future as well, given the major cost of transferring materials to electronic format. Delivery systems within consortia therefore have become another significant aspect of consortial efforts. Although some consortia have provided such delivery for some time on a more limited basis, such as the central areas of the Library Councils in New York State, delivery systems over a wider geographic scale are a more recent development. California's MELVYL system has been one of the first, with some other states following. Here in New York State, SUNY's SUNYConnect project includes a plan to develop a statewide union catalog and delivery system. Given the large number of institutions that are part of the SUNY system, 64 units total, the opening up of resources makes for a very exciting future for institutions involved, as well as undoubtedly much complexity and detail to work out. The expansion of these delivery systems to provide more efficient direct delivery of material to the distance learner might be difficult, but perhaps delivery could be done to a local library such as a public library, located closer geographically to the patron, rather than to their campus library, which could be quite some distance away or which then must turn around and mail material to the patron, adding to delivery time and expense.

Support for staff and group training is another increasing role of consortia in the new age (Bostick, 2001). Many times the cost of such training is more than an individual library can afford, thus the concept of providing strong training located closer geographically to libraries allows for better learning opportunities for librarians and staff. Group training opportunities for new techniques for providing services to distance learners could be emphasized in the future.

Teleconferences are another type of activity that consortia can become more involved with (Bostick, 2001). In addition to expanding the learning opportunities for librarians, teleconferences might eventually be sponsored by consortia for distance education students, to be shared by many campuses at once. Certainly, they are an excellent means for librarians to learn and discuss techniques for providing assistance to distance learners. Training sessions by video or computer CD ROM is one possible expansion of this idea. Work that is cooperatively shared in developing a video, or Web tutorial, on the use of a particular database or resource is more cost effective, and easier to keep up to date as the database changes.

One major role that consortia can increasingly help with is that of change management. Noam's article in *Science* discusses the old information flows that began about 5,000 to 8,000 years ago, where the model was "centrally stored information, scholars coming to the information, and a wide range of information subjects housed under one institutional roof" (Noam, 1995). Now the direction of information flow has reversed somewhat, and coping with the new changes after so many years of the same tradition is extremely difficult for libraries. Dealing with the fast pace of change is one of the most difficult things libraries face in the present day. As Hirshon comments in a recent article, "One of the most complex issues facing libraries today is change management. The decisions libraries face are becoming more complex, the risks are greater, and the resources–both human and fiscal–are becoming more scarce. There are many key issues facing libraries today that relate to the ability of the library to allocate and make maximum use of these scarce resources" (Hirshon, 1999). He also indicates that the elements of services, content management, organizational change, and technology demands are all aspects that consortia can assist with, especially as consortia have access to wide expertise. He goes on to comment "Library consortia will become even more important in the future by assisting libraries in implementing and managing the *process* of change. If libraries are unable to cope with and manage the process of change then all of the other tasks that are before it will become insurmountable. . . . A library consortium, with a broad understanding of how each of its members is coping with these issues, has an ideal opportunity to explore these issues objectively, to understand and articulate trends as they are emerging, and to create standardized methodologies that individual libraries can employ and customize at their own institutions." Hirshon also suggests the development of consultation services, to help libraries in their struggles to cope with new resources and new ways of providing service. Helping libraries with planning and coping will hopefully result in their better ability to provide organized and broad resources and services, especially for distance students.

One excellent example of cooperative planning is the formation of CETUS, Consortium for Educational Technology for University Systems. This group includes three of the largest programs in higher education, California State University (CSU), City University of New York (CUNY), and State University of New York (SUNY). Their alliance is a model for cooperative exploration of common problems and providing possible guides to solutions, and thus, has been an important thrust (Scepanski, 1998). One of CETUS's resulting publications, *Information Resources and Library Services for Distance Learners: A Framework for Quality* formulation (Consortium for Educational Technology for University Systems, 1997), contains several important sections, including a section titled *Information Resources and Library Services to Distance Learners: Statement of Principles*. The principles stated are as follows:

1. All faculty and students are entitled to an academically appropriate level of information resources and library resources no matter where or how the instruction is delivered.

2. Effective instruction requires collaboration among discipline faculty, librarians, and media/technology professionals in both the development and implementation of instructional programs.
3. Distance learning programs must include the development of relevant information competencies by all learners.
4. Appropriate access to information resources for distance learners requires a designated librarian facilitate the provision of information resources and library services for those students.
5. Effective distance learning requires broad application of the principles of fair use of copyrighted works, as well as other public rights of use of copyrighted works.
6. Commitment of resources and services for acquiring and distributing information is essential to planning and implementing distance learning programs.
7. Telecommunications and technology infrastructures must be reliable, ubiquitous, secure and supportive of distance learning programs.
8. Learners share responsibility with colleges and universities they attend for acquiring those tools and applications needed to access information resources.
9. Professional Schools of Library and Information Science should incorporate teaching and learning experiences on library services for distance learners.
10. Library collections and services should address unique learning styles among distance learners.
11. College and university academic administrators, librarians and faculty should institutionalize ongoing assessment of the quality of library services for their distance learners.
12. Learners must be made aware of unique academic, technology, and library requirements for the distance learning course(s) in which they are enrolled.

In addition to these statements of principles, recommendations for implementation are given as a guide to libraries, as well as a template for policy. Consortial work such as this involving the formation of guidelines and solutions will continue to be of vital importance, but it is clear from the content of these principles that consortia will also have to play a role in helping libraries accomplish the provision of these services for distance learners, given the extensive nature of what is needed.

Another area of important consortial activity is cataloging and intellectual access. This type of cooperation has been going on for quite some time, as pointed out earlier, but with the advent of electronic resources, this makes even more sense. Many vendors are supplying bibliographic records for their electronic resources, but since many libraries within a consortia purchase the same package, it makes perfect sense for the bibliographic records to be loaded into systems by the consortia where possible. It is of great help to patrons, especially distance patrons with less access to help from a reference librarian, to be able to link from the online catalog to these resources. Smaller libraries may also not have enough cataloging staff to be able to afford extensive cataloging of electronic resources. With consortial pressure, the quality of the bibliographic records hopefully can be high, providing the important access points that patrons need.

HEADING INTO THE FUTURE: PROBLEMS AS WELL AS SOLUTIONS

With the excitement and pleasure of the host of new possibilities for resource sharing comes also a truckload of new problems. The complexities of developing appropriate resolutions may take quite some time to accomplish.

One of the first problems is that of possible vendor instabilities. In today's world, companies and vendors can go under just as fast as they previously rose to instant success. There may be some security in numbers, so perhaps as vendors form their own equivalents of consortia, and they work more closely with library consortia, the risk factor for all may be decreased. In terms of support for distance education, libraries are counting most heavily on electronic resources for student support, so the importance of success of vendors and their products, as well as the success of library consortia that help them afford these resources, is significant. Consortia at times make it easier for vendors to survive by sending consolidated orders and payment to vendors for libraries in their consortia, providing technical and troubleshooting support that ease the burden for vendors, and sometimes in promoting good quality products (Sloan, 2000).

Another form of instability exists with the overnight changes that vendors sometimes make with little or no warning. Even when librarians are alerted to such changes with prior notice, there are few good ways to inform patrons other than when they make a contact for a query, either in person or by other means. Manoff indicates today's buzzwords for this as "content instability" and "content erosion" (Manoff, 2000). For distance learners, this can be tremendously confusing when search screens suddenly change, or when information they knew to be in the database seems to disappear when they go to use it again, with no librarian present to provide an explanation. As everyone knows, there is usually more strength in greater numbers, and here again, the pressure of consortia may make some progress with vendors, where surely one library's attempts alone would have no impact. As Morgan comments, "Consortia allow us to speak with a voice of authority rather than with a murmur" (Morgan, 1998).

Reciprocal borrowing agreements within particular groups or consortia expanded the availability of library resources in the past to patrons in the participating libraries. This was easy to accomplish when dealing with print resources, but with the shift of many collections to computerized resources, it may become more difficult to maintain the same level of sharing of resources. As the world of cooperation expands, some colleges and universities have placed further limits in terms of reciprocal borrowing of their print material on-site, and for many years, some have severely limited their lending of materials on interlibrary loan, even for a charge. Although some libraries may still allow access to their electronic resources to anyone unaffiliated with their campus on-site, not all libraries are willing to do so, and even where allowed, high use of computers located directly within library walls may make it difficult for students and faculty from other campuses to gain easy use, especially if higher priority is given to a campus affiliated patron, as is reasonable. Distance students without a home computer may therefore find it difficult to easily access the electronic resources that they need to accomplish their work.

As more and different consortia enter into joint purchases and other joint services, more and more overlap of offered items and services may occur. This results in less efficiency in the purchase of services, and more difficult decision making for each library. As Oder states, "librarians–especially those at large academic libraries–may find themselves faced with multiple, overlapping consortial relationships that strain their time and attention" (Oder, 2000). The resulting complexities can be difficult to deal with, as well as time consuming, as the playing field changes continually and each library must frequently re-evaluate how and what they purchase with whom. New roles of consortia could include important planning and training for selection techniques in terms of collection development with newer resources. They could also include cooperative development of policy as well, as the way students learn changes and new policies reflecting the changing nature of higher education are needed. It may be that, eventually, consortia will become increasingly involved with more aspects of collection development itself, rather than individual libraries. This places more control at the consortial level, and less with the individual library. As Inger states, "the members give up their ability to customize the packages and to influence platform and delivery issues" (Inger, 2000). Layering of consortia already exists in some instances, and it may be that eventually some of the overlap of consortia will be replaced with more layering for greater efficiency. Just one example of the existing layering is the New York Consortium of Consortia, which is "composed of fourteen member consortia, and it in turn belongs to larger groups such as the I.C.O.L.C. (International Coalition of Library Consortia)" (Landesman, 2000). Peters even discusses outsourcing of consortial services, which he calls "Consortium-to-consortium (C2C) services," to third parties, some of which are for-profit companies (Peters, 2001).

Using my own institution of SUNY Potsdam as an example, even four year colleges experience sizeable overlap. As part of the State University of New York system, we have opportunities provided by the Office of Library and Information Services, including the recent SUNYConnect initiatives. These initiatives include not only the forthcoming efforts for a jointly purchased online system, Exlibris's Aleph500 system, and the development of a statewide union catalog of holdings, along with plans for an accompanying delivery system, but also includes opportunities for joint purchase of electronic resources for SUNY campuses. However, we also have joint opportunities for purchase of electronic resources through NyLink, a statewide organization including all kinds of libraries, EmpireLink, an organization of New York State Library with similar types of libraries included, and our regional network, Northern New York Library Network. Some of the resources available for purchase through these different consortia do indeed overlap.

As different packages and bargain offers are offered from one year to the next by different consortia that an individual library is involved with, some databases in use may be replaced with different interfaces as pricing offers change. While this is difficult enough for students on campus to deal with in terms of these changes in interfaces for resources they use, it is even harder for distance students who may have no way of being alerted and no reference librarian in person to help explain the new search mechanism.

As part of the overlapping problem and escalation of electronic resources, licensing issues become more and more complex. Most individual libraries simply don't have enough staff and knowledge to deal with this complexity at a high volume. This is yet another way the consortia can lend support and help to libraries that may otherwise not have the capability to deal with the licensing and thus offer electronic resources for their users. One example is SO-LINET (Southeastern Library Network) and their Library Products & Services Program. With the need for libraries to handle more licenses in less time, SOLINET has moved their "licensing program away from more general, commodity-oriented, group discount products and toward unique databases that include a cost-recovery element from the vendor or library" (Baker, 2000). In addition, the consortia "provides central accounting, billing, and consulting services for licensing activities in the region." The overlapping of licenses still exists, but they are making progress, and they have also been able to solve some logistical problems, such as different fiscal year time periods among member libraries. Although licensing agreements may become more complex as numbers in a group increase, time may also be saved on licensing agreements and purchasing arrangements in the process. Especially in consortia that are large enough to include consortia staff, or even member staff with the knowledge and expertise to do the work more easily, this will be of significant benefit to all. The resulting time savings may allow libraries to shift more of their staffing into assisting patrons, and the sometimes more time consuming process of assisting distance students.

One increasing problem is the tendency of distance students, not to mention students on campus, to rely solely on electronic resources that are available fulltext. As Saunders comments, "Digital technology has changed people's concept of time. Because computers retrieve and process information rapidly, users expect speed in all aspects of their lives, including their transactions with the library" (Saunders, 1999). With today's world being that of more instant gratification, students may block out other excellent resources simply because they are not available fulltext online anywhere and students are reluctant to wait for a print copy. Desktop document delivery may help some, but there are too many books and other resources to ever dream that all text would ever become virtual, at least for quite some years to come. Overreliance on Web resources with not enough evaluation of resources by students is a problem as well, although it should be noted that students many times in the past were not all that knowledgeable or careful about evaluation of print sources either. As Landesman comments in his article, "we know that what is online will be used whether or not it was used before and regardless of its quality. This is a phenomenon that alarms librarians, though there is nothing new about it. Users have always taken the path of least resistance" (Landesman, 2000).

One major problem, especially for distance students who may have no other alternative, is that of downtime when electronic resources cannot be accessed. When either a part of the connecting Internet loop or the vendor site is down, access to resources can be totally gone. If the downtime is of greater length, distance students are without any of their usual resources for their library research. The importance of stable infrastructures cannot be overemphasized, and perhaps consortial activity needs to expand more into this area as well. Allen emphasizes the importance of shifting funds from process to services and "the need to invest (and continually re-invest) in a network infrastructure capable of meeting demand for the delivery of digital information" (Allen,1999).

An additional problem for distance students related to the above is their being blocked from use of electronic resources because of a problem with the campus proxy server and/or a problem with their username and password not allowing them proper access to the resources. This circumstance struck home for me personally when I received a long distance phone call from a distance student in the United Kingdom who was having this problem while I was serving on the reference desk one weekend. The idea of 24-hour access to resources becomes even more important when we begin to have students that are crossing countries and time zones.

Crossing countries becomes even more complex when college programs themselves cross the borders. Our own campus, SUNY Potsdam, is considering offering a graduate program at a satellite site in Canada in Ottawa, Ontario, given Canadian needs for more programs offering graduate degrees in particular areas of the field of education. The problems of providing library services in a different nation seem daunting, especially with Canadian mails being hopelessly slow in terms of mailing books to patrons somewhat like interlibrary loan and in terms of how to provide adequate reference service.

One important aspect of support for distance learners is still the assistance of the reference librarian. Phone service, email, and instant messenger type services are the most prevalent means of support for distance reference service at present. However, this kind of service many times is more difficult than service provided in person. Studies have shown that "missing or incomplete information was the biggest problem" in virtual reference situations and that "users sometimes omitted information that was essential to answering a query, and staff sometimes omitted essential information in answering queries" (Sloan, 1998). This sometimes also happens with in-person reference interviews, but usually is easier to spot and resolve. There are times when in-person assistance and instruction are still the best means for providing help. Also, as Cooper, Dempsey, and Menon comment, many faculty expect their students to use a library for their resources, whether they are students on campus or distance learners (Cooper, 1998), so libraries need to somehow provide for that need. As part of SUNY Potsdam's involvement in the Fort Drum Consortium and our offering of distance education classes in the Watertown region, our campus participates along with other institutions in combined support of two part-time librarian positions in the library at Jefferson Community College in Watertown. JCC is a sister community college in the SUNY system, so it makes sense to use this tie for better support of distance students from SUNY Potsdam and other campuses involved in the consortium. The Fort Drum Consortium also sometimes provides support for information resources as well, with the purchase of materials to be housed at JCC in support of consortia classes. At one point a few years ago, our library purchased an ERIC CD-ROM index on SilverPlatter to be housed at JCC for use by SUNY Potsdam off campus students. Another example involving our own institution has been a cooperative venture with SUNY Plattsburgh and their distance Telenursing Program. SUNY Plattsburgh purchased a computer and printer at one point that was housed in our library at SUNY Potsdam, as well as a small number of print reference materials, with our reference librarians assisting Plattsburgh students in their needs. As time has gone on, however, the need for assisting students has dropped to near zero as more distance students own computers themselves and access their needs directly from home. These types of models may be useful for consortia to consider in the future, to expand available reference assistance to students by funding librarians in various locations. Bridges points out that academia is deluged at present with business models for campuses, which don't always work well for academic institutions. He indicates that face to face reference is still very valuable, and he emphasizes that in the race to go with the newest, good library service shouldn't be forgotten (Bridges, 2001).

As the need for virtual reference service increases, it may be difficult for libraries to provide enough staffing for this newer means of reference on their own. Consortia may find themselves wandering into this area of cooperative sharing as well. It may be that consortia could hire reference librarians for a group of campuses, with students from those campuses contacting one central point for assistance with their needs, rather than just interacting with their own campus. Such models do exist with projects such as Virtual Reference Desk AskA Consortium, which is geared to the K-12 education community (Kasowitz, 2000). The existing models work in different ways. Within some models queries go to one expert in a subject area and in other cases, all overflow questions that can't be dealt with promptly, regardless of the topic, go to a cooperative digital reference service. Kasowitz also cites Lankes' twelve quality characteristics of digital reference service, which are: authoritative; accessible; fast (turnaround of response); private (protects user information); consistent with good reference practice; clear in user expectations; reviewed regularly; provides access to related information; noncommercial; publicized; instructive; and offers training to experts (meaning the reference providers). Although providing cooperative digital reference service at the academic level may be more complex and difficult, effective services could be developed over time. We may begin to see more of the virtual librarian, along with the virtual library. As vendors and consortia-type vendor groups expand in size and service, it may also be that, down the road, the vendors themselves may hire reference librarians to provide virtual reference help with their specific databases. It will be very interesting to see what the reference world is like even ten years from now.

With the advent of video reference, the possibilities become even more complex. However, video reference for distance learners may have little use until well into the future. Most learners won't have easy access to the appropriate and expensive equipment, but are more apt to have a home computer for electronic reference use, or at least access to a computer closer to home. Studies have also shown that the technology is still new enough that problems with equipment still exist (Sloan, 1998).

Niemi, Ehrhard, and Neeley discuss another possibility for assisting distance learners, where librarians would "compose and distribute some standard research protocols for electronic information access" (Niemi, 1998). Because electronic resources are changing so fast, however, this could be a very time consuming process, and could perhaps be more efficient if done by group or consortial effort. Of course the most difficult problem still resulting is how to get patrons to actually read the information in today's busy world.

Whether the reference service is provided in person or virtually, it is wise to keep in mind that the technology is only a means to arrive at the information resources, and that librarians still play important roles for patrons, including distance patrons. Bridge's important comment should be remembered: "One has to ask whether it might produce better librarians to put less emphasis on their ability to create Web pages and more on their ability to think critically and be well-rounded individuals with diverse intellectual interests" (Bridges, 2001). Perhaps with ever changing technology and resources, Bridges is quite right to voice the importance of critical thinking as the true basis for good librarianship. Consortia can then later help librarians build their knowledge of newer technology and in providing better virtual reference.

Another problem still to be solved is how to better organize resources in today's changing world. With course management software such as Blackboard, yet another means of accessing information exists. As everything related to a particular course shifts to such software, the student becomes accustomed to finding their course syllabus, assignments, lab information, and class discussion there. They will also clearly expect that access to information resources will eventually appear there as well. At present, they mostly find an instructor's listing of resources, and many of the course software packages contain an information resources package, but usually they are of poor content and quality. Even leaving aside the issue of course management software and their complications for library service, organization of resources in terms of library OPACs and Websites still needs much thought and evaluation, given the tremendous changes in resources and how they are accessed in today's world. Certainly it is confusing enough for students on campus with in-person access to a librarian to understand where particular resources are and how to get to them, but it is even harder for distance learners to determine this on their own. Adding to the complexity for students is what Manoff terms the "hybridity" of electronic resources. She states: "Online catalogs and library Web pages begin to merge with electronic journals and full-text databases to which they connect. Patrons may find it difficult to distinguish catalogs from indexes, from full-text databases, from document delivery, from interlibrary loan, and even online reference" (Manoff, 2000). She goes on to point out that it becomes more and more difficult for a patron to determine what kind of material they have, or even "where a library's Web site ends and where resources mounted elsewhere begin." This confusion is difficult to resolve even with a librarian present sometimes, let alone for a patron removed at their own separate location and isolated from help. Web resources disappearing overnight is another sizeable problem, especially for distance students. It is difficult for them to understand when materials they have used for research disappear suddenly, leaving that trail of research lost. With today's movement toward access versus ownership, and at times connectivity rather than classification, the need for finding the best ways to organize access and materials is significant. Here again, consortia may be able to offer strong support to libraries in helping them accomplish this, or in some cases, accomplishing this for them.

The present day's fast paced lifestyle has also influenced the perceived need of patrons and as Quinn points out, "The fast-food concept of quick service may have had the effect of raising the expectations of library users" (Quinn, 2000). He also points out the different marketing strategies prevalent in higher education at this point are closer to business models, and thus "librarians must acquiesce by providing the 'Information Happy Meals' the students are seeking in order to guarantee 'customer satisfaction.'" The additional pressures of distance students may amplify this need for quick access and delivery of information resources related to their studies.

One result of the reliance on electronic resource packages is the nature and scope of resources becoming less diverse. Quinn sees this as a process of "McDonaldization" of collections, as is happening throughout higher education according to some of the literature. He states, "McDonald's meals are predictable because they offer uniform contents and preparation. Similarly, academic libraries offer increasingly predictable content resulting from the widespread use of approval plans to add books and of aggregator packages to add electronic databases and journals to the collection. The collection development process has become more and more standardized, resulting in collection content varying less from one library or type of library to another" (Quinn, 2000). Dickinson comments on the importance of continued individuality of collections and states, "it is not intuitively clear that a balanced collection is necessarily desirable. With ever-shrinking library budgets, one effect of an attempt to develop a balanced collection will be to distribute increasingly scarce resources over a constant or growing number of subject areas competing for support. The result of this situation, if continued for a sufficient amount of time, will be to produce an 'oatmeal' collection, i.e., one which, while perhaps extensive in subject coverage, is uniformly bland, shallow, and undistinguished" (Dickinson, 1989). Since distance students rely heavily on electronic resources and normally have a smaller number of resources available, they need to have access to more than just bland collections in support of their educational coursework.

As technology heads us deeper into a world totally dependent on the computer and media for information resources, this widens the gap between the haves and have nots. This starts in the younger grades, where young students with home computers have much more exposure to electronic resources than those students who only have access at school or public libraries. This seriously widens the gap between those with good knowledge of computers and those without, even before students enter the arena of higher education. For distance students, those who don't own a computer at home are placed at a significant loss compared with those that do. In addition, as the world shifts to desktop document delivery, one may expect that at some point, student patrons may have to begin to pay at least part of the high costs involved, as libraries become less able to absorb all costs as prices escalate and budgets remain stagnant. This will change the old model of access for all who "walk" in the library door, and again will result in a gap in the ability to obtain resources between those who can afford all the material that they need, and those who cannot. Hopefully, consortial efforts can also help to resolve this problem.

CONCLUSION

As distance learners become more and more prevalent in our institutions of higher education, the need for cooperative ventures in terms of resource sharing to support distance learning makes tremendous sense. As Bostick states, "Cooperation just to maintain the status quo has evolved into cooperation to redefine library collections and services. The future for library consortia is bright and exciting!" (Bostick, 2001). The initiation of a new column in *Journal of Academic Librarianship* on library consortia (Peters, 2001) is yet more evidence of the important role that consortia are expected to play in academic libraries in the future.

For distance learners, access to a wider array of resources and services for their information needs rests heavily on consortia. As the world of consortia expands, libraries may well think more often in collective terms rather than individual terms. As Kyrillidou comments on the future for international cooperation, "it is imperative that at least some institutions move the thinking about access to electronic resources *from* providing access to local users *to* providing access to users in general" (Kyrillidou, 1999). Landesman also comments that the library community "is growing closer as resource sharing blurs the distinctions among collections and distance education challenges the idea of an individual library's patrons" (Landesman, 2000). As distance learning becomes more prominent, libraries will have to move toward thinking of users as "ours," rather than "mine" and "yours." As Potter comments "services offered by these consortia are increasingly placeless and virtual" (Potter, 1997), and thus, patrons and especially distance patrons also may be virtual too.

Alexander views the present time frame as the next "important milestone in library cooperative activities" since the beginnings around a hundred years ago (Alexander, 1999). It is clear that the time is ripe for action in terms of increasing cooperation of libraries to achieve success with the new expectations of information seekers, and especially, distance learners.

REFERENCES

Association of College and Research Libraries. Distance Learning Section Guidelines Committee. (2000) "Guidelines for Distance Learning Library Services," *College & Research Libraries News* 61 (11): 1023-1029.

Alexander, Adrian W. (1999) "Toward 'The Perfection of Work': Library Consortia in the Digital Age," *Journal of Library Administration* 28 (2): 1-14.

Allen, Barbara McFadden. (1999), "Consortia and Collections: Achieving a Balance Between Local Action and Collaborative Interest," *Journal of Library Administration* 28 (4): 85-90.

Allen, Barbara McFadden & Hirshon, Arnold. (1998) "Hanging Together to Avoid Hanging Separately: Opportunities for Academic Libraries and Consortia," *Information Technology and Libraries* 17 (1): 36-44.

Baker, Angee. (2000) "The Impact of CONSORTIA on Database Licensing," *Computers in Libraries* 20 (6): 46-50.

Balas, Janet. (1998) "Library Consortia in the Brave New Online World," *Computers in Libraries* 18 (4): 42-44.

Bostick, Sharon L. (2001) "The History and Development of Academic Library Consortia in the United States: An Overview," *Journal of Academic Librarianship* 27 (2): 128-130.

Bridges, Karl. (2001) "Why Traditional Librarianship Matters," *American Libraries* 32 (10): 52-54.

Carr, Reg. (1998) "Research Collections in the Digital Age: the Role of CURL," *Library Review* 47 (5/6): 277-281.

Cary, Karen & Ogburn, Joyce L. (2000) "Developing a Consortial Approach to Cataloging and Intellectual Access," *Library Collections, Acquisitions, and Technical Services* 24 (2000): 45-51.

Connolly, Pauline, & Reidy, Denis, eds. (2000) *The Digital Library: Challenges and Solutions For the New Millennium.* Boston Spa, United Kingdom: IFLA Offices for UAP and International Lending.

Consortium for Educational Technology for University Systems. (1997) *Information Resources and Library Services for Distance Learners: A Framework for Quality.* Seal Beach, CA: Trustees of California State University.

Curtis, Donnelyn & Stoll, Karen. (2000) "Partners in Supporting Science: Academic and Government Research Libraries," *Government Information Quarterly* 17 (3): 291-298.

Dannelly, Gay N. " 'Uneasy Lies the Head': Selecting Resources in a Consortial Setting," *Journal of Library Administration* 28 (2): 57-67.

Dickinson, Dennis W. (1989) "A Rationalist's Critique of Book Selection for Academic Libraries," in Gorman, B.B. and B.R. Howes *Collection Development for Libraries.* London: Bowker-Saur: 214-224.

Gayas-ud-din (1993) "Information Networks and Systems in India," *Resource Sharing and Information Networks* 8 (2): 119-125.

Giordano, Tommaso. "Digital Resource Sharing and Library Consortia in Italy," *Information Technology and Libraries* 19 (2): 84-89.

Hirshon, Arnold. (1999) "Libraries, Consortia, and Change Management," *Journal of Academic Librarianship* 25 (2): 124-126.

Inger, Simon, Kusma, Taissa, & Allen, Barbara McFadden. (2000) "The Pricing Implications of Site and Consortia Licensing into the Next Millennium," *The Serials Librarian* 38 (3/4): 219-224.

International Coalition of Library Consortia. (1998) "Statement of Current Perspective and Preferred Practices for the Selection and Purchase of Electronic Information," *Information Technology and Libraries* 17 (1): 45-50.

Kasowitz, Abby, Bennett, Blythe, & Lankes, R. David. (2000) "Quality Standards for Digital Reference Consortia," *Reference and User Services Quarterly* 39 (4): 355-363.

Ke, Hao-Ren & Chang, Ruei-Chuan. (2000) "Resource Sharing Digital Libraries: A Case Study of Taiwan's InfoSpring Digital Library Project," *Library Collections, Acquisitions, and Technical Services* 24 (3): 371-377.

Kochan, Carol A. & Lee, Daniel R. (1998) "Utah Article Delivery: A New Model for Consortial Resource Sharing," *Computers in Libraries* 18 (4): 24-28.

Kopp, James J. (1998) "Library Consortia and Information Technology: The Past, the Present, the Promise," *Information Technology and Libraries* 17 (1): 7-12.

Kyrillidou, Martha. (1999) "New Collections: New Marketplace Relationships," *Resource Sharing & Information Networks* 14 (1): 61-75.

Landesman, Margaret & Van Reenen, Johann. (2000) "Consortia vs. Reform: Creating Congruence," *JEP: The Journal of Electronic Publishing* 6 (2): Available http://www.press.umich.edu/jep/06-02/landesman.html.

Manoff, Marlene. (2000) "Hybridity, Mutability, Multiplicity: Theorizing Electronic Library Collections," *Library Trends* 48 (4): 857-876.

Michalak, Sarah C. (2000) "The Evolution of SPARC," *Serials Review* 26 (1): 10-21.

Morgan, Eric Lease. (1998) "Resource Sharing and Consortia, or, Becoming a 600-Pound Gorilla," *Computers in Libraries* 18 (4): 40-41.

Niemi, John A., Ehrhard, Barbara J., & Neeley, Lynn. (1998) "Off-Campus Library Support for Distance Adult Learners," *Library Trends* 47 (1): 65-74.

Noam, Eli M. (1995) "Electronics and the Dim Future of the University," *Science* 270 (5234): 247-249.

Oblinger, Diana G., Barone, Carole A. & Hawkins, Brian L. (2001) *Distributed Education and Its Challenges: An Overview.* Washington, D.C.: American Council on Education Center for Policy Analysis.

Oder, Norman. (2000) "Consortia Hit Critical Mass," *Library Journal* 125 (2): 48-51.

Payne, Lizanne. (1998) "The Washington Research Library Consortium: A Real Organization for a Virtual Library," *Information Technology and Libraries* 17 (1): 13-17.

Peters, Thomas A. (2001) "Consortia Speaking: Agile Innovation Clubs," *Journal of Academic Librarianship* 27 (2): 149-151.

Potter, William Gray. (1997) "Recent Trends in Statewide Academic Library Consortia," *Library Trends* 45 (3): 416-34.

Quinn, Brain. (2000) "The McDonaldization of Academic Libraries?" *College and Research Libraries* 61 (3): 248-261.

Reibel, Iris. (2000) "Couperin: Un Exemple de Consortium pour la Fourniture Electronique des Documents," *Bulletin d'Informations de L' Association des Bibliothecaires Francais* 188: 94-95.

Rogers, Michael. (1994) "SUNY/CUNY Combine Index Resources via NOTIS PACLink," *Library Journal* 119 (14): 131.

Rohe, Terry Ann, O'Donovan, Patrice & Hanawalt, Victoria. (2000) "Cooperative Collection Development in PORTALS," *The Acquisitions Librarian*, 24: 89-101.

Saunders, Laverna M. (1999) "The Human Element in the Virtual Library," *Library Trends* 47 (4): 771-787.

Scepanski, Jordan M. & von Wahlde, Barbara. (1998) "Megasystem Collaboration: Cross-Continent Consortial Cooperation," *Information Technology and Libraries* 17 (1): 30-35.

"ScienceDirect Launches Consortium in China," (2000) *Computers in Libraries* 20 (6): 10.

Simpson, Donald B. (1998) "Economics of Cooperative Collection Development and Management: The United States' Experience with Rarely Held Research Materials," *IFLA Journal* 24 (3): 161-165.

Sloan, Bernie. (1998) "Service Perspectives for the Digital Library Remote Reference Services," *Library Trends* 47 (1): 117-143.

Sloan, Bernie. (2000) "Understanding Consortia Better: What Vendors Can Learn," *Library Journal* 125 (5): 57-58.

"SPARC Collaborates on BioOne for Full-Text Access," (1999) *Computers in Libraries* 19 (8): 58.

Thornton, Glenda A. (2000) "Impact of Electronic Resources on Collection Development, the Roles of Librarians, and Library Consortia," *Library Trends* 48 (4): 842-856.

Tonta, Yasar. (2001) "Collection Development of Electronic Information Resources in Turkish University Libraries," *Library Collections, Acquisitions, and Technical Services* 25 (3): 291-298.

Wiley, Lynn & Chrzastowski, Tina E. (2001) "The State of ILL in the State of IL: The Illinois Interlibrary Loan Assessment Project," *Library Collections, Acquisitions, and Technical Services* 25 (1): 5-20.

Williams, Bernard. (1997) "Document Delivery Survey, Winter 1997," *FID News Bulletin* 47 (11/12): 293-296.

Instructional Services
for Distance Education

Robin Kinder

SUMMARY. Instructional services in libraries need new technologies and new models for assisting distance learners. This article presents ACRL guidelines for library instruction and services for distance education; the lack of service issues addressed in digital library discussions; distance students' characteristics; the central role the library liaison will play to distance students; and remote service as a primary service to distance users. *[Article copies available for a fee from The Haworth Document Delivery Service: 1-800-HAWORTH. E-mail address: <getinfo@haworthpressinc. com> Website: <http://www.HaworthPress.com> © 2002 by The Haworth Press, Inc. All rights reserved.]*

KEYWORDS. Distance learners, library instructional services, ACRL guidelines, library instruction

The missing element of library services in distance education has become a major concern in the field and in the professional literature. The focus of the past several years on digital library implementation and collections and on acquisitions of electronic resources has overshadowed the need for service, particularly instructional services. The dominance of the digital library in the

Robin Kinder is Reference Librarian, William Allan Neilson Library, Smith College, Northampton, MA 01063 (E-mail: rkinder@smith.edu). She is currently enrolled in the doctoral program in information science at SUNY Albany.

[Haworth co-indexing entry note]: "Instructional Services for Distance Education." Kinder, Robin. Co-published simultaneously in *The Reference Librarian* (The Haworth Information Press, an imprint of The Haworth Press, Inc.) No. 77, 2002, pp. 63-70; and: *Distance Learning: Information Access and Services for Virtual Users* (ed: Hemalata Iyer) The Haworth Information Press, an imprint of The Haworth Press, Inc., 2002, pp. 63-70. Single or multiple copies of this article are available for a fee from The Haworth Document Delivery Service [1-800-HAWORTH, 9:00 a.m. - 5:00 p.m. (EST). E-mail address: getinfo@haworthpressinc. com].

professional literature cannot be underestimated. "Much has been written about the digital library. The focus of most studies, papers, and articles has been on the technology or on the types of resources offered. Human interaction in the digital library is discussed far less frequently. One would almost get the impression that the service tradition of the physical library will be unnecessary and redundant in the digital library environment." Sloan explores the many definitions of digital library in the literature, concluding that most definitions have "an emphasis on technology and information resources and a very noticeable lack of discussion of the service aspects of the digital library" (Sloan 1998, 117, 119).

The Association of the College and Research Libraries (ACRL) Standards and Accreditation Committee (SAC) revised its 1990 guidelines for extended campus library services in 1998. The ACRL *Guidelines for Distance Learning Library Services* addresses instruction as philosophy:

- The instilling of lifelong learning skills through general bibliographic and information literacy instruction in academic libraries is a primary outcome of higher education. Such preparation and measurement of its outcomes are of equal necessity for the distance learning community as for those on the traditional campus.

And as service:

- A program of library user instruction designed to instill independent and effective information literacy skills while specifically meeting the learner-support needs of the distance learning community
- Assistance with and instruction in the use of nonprint media and equipment (ACRL/SAC 1998).

It is important that distance education librarians be aware as well of the *Guidelines for Instruction Programs in Academic Libraries* (2000), *Objectives for Information Literacy Instruction: A Model Statement for Academic Librarians* (2001), and *Information Literacy Competency Standards for Higher Education* (2000). Due to the adoption of distance education in many academic institutions, instructional and distance education librarians need these guidelines for creating a substantial and equal program of instruction for distance learners.

WHERE IS INSTRUCTION?

Providing reference services and providing instruction may occur simultaneously with individuals in the physical library, but instruction for distance users must be purposefully programmed and designed with the same commitment given to traditional class instruction. Services such as email and chat are more immediately reference services; they do not serve instructional needs as well, although chat holds the most potential as an available, low-cost method of instruction. The nature of chat or instant messaging implies that the interchange is swifter, while email is more perfunctory. In a recent article, Viggiano and Ault describe the difficulties of providing online chat instruction in a classroom setting, including increased complexity in teaching content and technology simultaneously to new students and delays in assuring full class participation at any given point. Instead, multiple sessions with fewer than ten students are advisable (Viggiano and Ault 2001, 138). Using chat as a virtual classroom, however, is an opportunity for librarians to move beyond traditional methods to address the needs of distance learners.

While distance education students may have access to local libraries, the home institution and its resources and services will be most heavily relied upon. Access to electronic databases, interlibrary loan, document delivery, and reference services and instruction are critical components in the process of creating skilled, lifelong learners. The recent emphasis on information literacy compounds the issue of instruction. How will distance education students receive instruction and become lifelong, skilled information seekers?

While libraries have made progress in acquiring and providing access to resources and collections, providing an instructional component to a library's Web pages is less easily accomplished. It is understandable that librarians gave priority to acquiring and providing access to digital collections, full-text resources and bibliographic databases, but the instructional aspect is absent from most library Web pages.

In an article in response to Bill Miller's critical article of reference services, David Tyckoson posited that Miller's idea of mapping knowledge had always been done by librarians in the form of bibliographies, pathfinders, handouts and, now, Web pages (Tyckoson 1999). Libraries' subject Web pages typically do resemble print bibliographies; the difference is only in the access. Print bibliographies and pathfinders created by librarians were passive artifacts stored on a display rack. Creating an electronic version makes it accessible, but no more active or engaging to the end user than print. For instance, subject resource pages allow access to catalogs, databases, digital collections and Internet sites, but still resemble an electronic display rack. Providing instruction in search strategies, selection of resources and use of resources is as absent from electronic pathfinders as they were from their print counterparts. Carr-Chellman and Philip Duchastel note in a recent article: "It is not enough to simply transpose traditional courses to the new medium of the Web in order to create an online institution. This will not take advantage of the opportunities of the Web. There are many unfortunate instances on the Web where such transposition leads to a stilted use of this medium for instructional purposes. It needs to be recognized that online education is a specific medium in its own right and thus, it will have its own design considerations for effective instruction" (Carr-Chellman and Duchastel 2001, 145). While the authors are referring to a university level online course, the portrayal may apply to forcing print traditions onto electronic mediums. Librarians are as mistaken as institutional leaders to equate access with learning, that is, when institutional leaders believe that distance students' electronic access to the library is the end of the story. Considering a new medium, particularly a visual medium, has not been a strength of reference services. The difficulty in designing visual learning spaces on a library Web page is likely due to a lack of resources within a library, lack of access to technology, and a reliance on more traditional methods of communication, such as subject resource pages that are, essentially, the old pathfinders. While technology is a critical component in providing distance instruction, the library's needs for instruction can be folded into the framework provided for faculty in teaching distance students. If a class were taught by broadcast satellite, then librarians would negotiate with faculty to provide instruction via satellite, focusing on content rather than transmission, software and hardware. Meola and Stormont (2000) provide an overview of current technology for reference services, some of which are adaptable to instruction, particularly chat and collaborative software. This article is concerned primarily with instruction to distance users, rather than technology, and the cautionary hope that librarians will not consider existing Web pages, even subject pages, to be adequate for distance users.

DISTANCE LEARNERS AND PROVIDERS

Adult learners may be characterized as somewhat similar to remote users, as experienced in life and work, focused in goal setting, motivated, knowledgeable about technology, and requiring education in "intense doses" due to time limitations (Niemi and Ehrhard 1998; Cooper and Dempsey 1998). This characterization is extremely fluid as the distance education population grows. Within a few years, there may be no way to define distance learners and, at some critical point in time, most librarians will be involved in distance teaching, primarily because on-campus users are often distant from the physical library, and as such, become a variation on the distance learner in a formal distance program. Providing reference services to remote users via telephone, email and chat is at present the primary conduit for instruction. Certainly, more advanced technologies for distance education will be incorporated into the library's methods of instruction within the next few years.

Cooper and Dempsey list six implications for staff in libraries when providing services to distance learners, including identification and service to a discrete group, conducting focus groups and interviews to gauge needs, and establishing relationships with other libraries, as well as informing distance students of services from both home and local libraries (Cooper and Dempsey, 1998). It needs to be stated strongly, however, that identifying distant students as a discrete group should not result in a lessening or reduction in library service. Lebowitz cautions that library services to distant students is an equity issue, one in which both administrators and librarians may focus too fully on their own interests, such as accreditation and access or instruction, respectively. "When developing library services for off-campus/distance education students, it is necessary to consider all aspects: accreditation, guidelines for services, institutional commitment and institutional and student environment" (Lebowitz 1997, 304).

ADDRESSING THE ISSUES

The development of distance education programs is a collaborative effort between administration and faculty, information technology and media services, and the library. While the administration will seek to constrain costs and information technology may demand staff, the library may fail to demand equal access to technology and staff. A dedicated librarian in a distance education program is ideal as the center of three groups: distance users, technology staff, and librarians. It would be extremely difficult for a subject specialist to be designated the liaison to distance education, due to the varying demands of distance education users. Equally problematic would be no designated liaison, carrying with it the assumption that reference services can merely add distance instruction to its tasks and responsibilities. Adopting such a course would result in each librarian negotiating between individual faculty and technology staff, duplicating many times over the learning and experiences of librarians in reaching distant students. Such a course of action would likely lead to inequities of service to distance users. Eventually, a remote services librarian serving all off-campus constituencies would be the likely outcome of any scenario involving distance.

In a liaison role only, the need is for a professional librarian to be the liaison to information technology and the library, regardless of position. For instance, a cataloger or interlibrary loan librarian could be the designated remote services librarian with liaison responsibilities to information technology and subject librarians who teach with faculty. The remote services position would be instrumental in developing and maintaining the liaison role between remote users, campus constituents, and the library. Insisting that only reference can provide a relationship to distance students would be repeating the mistake that only reference librarians can create Web sites, when catalogers were overlooked in their expert knowledge of classifying information. Regardless of which person or position is designated, the crucial ingredient would be actually designating a librarian to indicate the importance of the endeavor, the library's service imperative and the needs of the distance student.

FURTHER READING

Libraries who are currently adopting or will be adopting distance education programs may want to read the Fall 2000 *Library Trends* issue on *Assessing Digital Library Services*. This issue contains the case study for the Alexandria Digital Earth Prototype (ADEPT), a fascinating look at a five-year project to deploy geo-referenced information to undergraduate students. It is mistaken to ignore this study due to its subject specificity: the final report will likely contain a wealth of information for all aspects of teaching and learning using format- and information-rich resources, particularly the use of digital libraries and visualization to enhance learning. From Gorman's study of "bundles," or organized packets of information, to Carter and Janes' examination of digital reference questions, the lines and lessons are blurring between what can be learned from studying digital libraries and what has been learned from studying physical libraries. Another journal issue dedicated to distance education is *The Reference Librarian* (2000) on *Library Outreach, Partnership and Distance Education: Reference Librarians at the Gateway*. Technology, specific user groups–such as minority cultural centers–and new user programs and outreach services are identified as components of distance education. Of particular note is Casper's "Outreach to Distance Learners: When the Distance Education Instructor Sends Students to the Library, Where Do They Go?" Additionally, *Library Trends'* (2001) computer assisted instruction issue contains Cox's "Teaching From the Web: Constructing a Library Learning Environment Where Connections Can Be Made." In recognition of the blurring lines between digital and physical libraries, librarians should anticipate the publication of *Digital Library Use: Social Practice in Design and Evaluation* by Ann Bishop, Barbara Buttenfield, and Nancy Van House. The use and evaluation of digital libraries informs us of user needs and expectations in ways traditional use and evaluation may have missed or never experienced. Issues of access, privacy, intellectual property, service and collections are now more critical for the digital library than for the physical library, and the new environments will create new questions and new answers for each. The digital library enhances the physical library, if developed properly, just as distance education may enhance the parent or virtual institution, if developed properly. The digital library will be *the library* for the remote user, however much one disagrees on its definition. In this environment, the digital library enhances the physical library, rather than detracts from, and the care given to the organization, access, and service in the physical library belongs as well in the digital library, including service philosophy and practice.

CONCLUSION

Adopting any one model of reference service becomes more difficult, as communities of library users expand beyond physical boundaries. Reference services now extend beyond the library, campus, or locality to a more diverse, even global, community. Unique digital collections bring new virtual users to the library that meet across space and time. Eventually, outside of formal distance education programs, the majority of users will be distant and the majority of librarians will be remote service librarians. Whether librarians simply provide answers to queries or seek to instruct users, service to the distance user should be an integral part of every library's mission and purpose.

REFERENCES

Arant, W and P.A. Mosley. (1999). Library Outreach, Partnerships, and Distance Education: Reference Librarians at the Gateway. *The Reference Librarian* 67/68: 1-311.

Carr-Chellman A. and P. Duchastel. (2001). The ideal online course. *Library Trends* 50: 145-160.

Cooper R. and P. Dempsey. (1998). Remote library users–needs and expectations. *Library Trends* 42: 145-160.

Guidelines for distance learning library services. www.ala.org/acrl/guides/distlgmg. html. (May 18, 2002).

Guidelines for instruction programs in academic libraries. www.ala.org/acrl/guides/ guiis.html (May 18, 2002).

Information literacy competency standards for higher education. www.ala.org/acrl/ ilstandardlo.html (May 18, 2002).

Lebowitz, G. (1997). Library services to distant students: an equity issue. *Journal of Academic Librarianship* 23: 303-308.

McFadden, T. (2001). Computer-based instruction in libraries and library education. *Library Trends* 50: 1-158.

Meola, M. and S. Stormont. (1999). Real-Time Reference Service for the Remote User: From the Telephone and Electronic Mail to Internet Chat, Instant Messaging, and Collaborative Software. *The Reference Librarian* 67/68: 29-51.

Objectives for information literacy instruction: A model statement for academic librarians. www.ala.org/acrl/guides/objinfolit.html (May 18, 2002).

Peters, T. (2000). Assessing Digital Library Services. *Library Trends*: 49: 221-385.

Sloan, B. (1998). Service perspectives for the digital library remote reference services. *Library Trends* 47: 117-43.

Niemi, J. A. and B. Ehrhard. (1998). Off campus library support for distance adult learners. *Library Trends* 47: 65-74.

Tyckoson, D. (1999). What's right with reference. *American Libraries* 30: 57-63.

Viggiano, R. and M. Ault. (2001). Online library instruction for online students. *Information Technology and Libraries* 20: 135-138.

Virtual Teaching:
Library Instruction via the Web

Carol Anne Germain
Gregory Bobish

SUMMARY. Instruction librarians are developing Web-based instruction tools, including interactive tutorials, to teach remote users and students enrolled in distance education programs. This mode of teaching requires a different approach than the traditional in-class bibliographic instruction, since face-to-face interaction is absent. Special attention is required during planning stages to compose quality library instruction Web resources.

This article outlines strategies librarians can incorporate to develop effective and functional Web-based tools. Topics that are addressed include page design and layout, technical and copyright issues, usability and evaluation, and site maintenance. Examples from the University at Albany's User Education Department are used to highlight these themes. The Texas Information Literacy Tutorial (TILT), a model interactive information literacy Web-based tutorial, is also reviewed. *[Article copies available for a fee from The Haworth Document Delivery Service: 1-800-HAWORTH. E-mail address: <getinfo@haworthpressinc.com> Website: <http://www. HaworthPress.com> © 2002 by The Haworth Press, Inc. All rights reserved.]*

KEYWORDS. Distance learning, Web sites, virtual reference services, Texas Information Literacy Tutorial

Carol Anne Germain is Networked Resources Education Librarian, University at Albany, University Library, UL-128, 1400 Washington Avenue, Albany, NY 12222 (E-mail: cg219@albany.edu). Gregory Bobish is User Education/Reference Librarian, University at Albany.

[Haworth co-indexing entry note]: "Virtual Teaching: Library Instruction via the Web." Germain, Carol Anne, and Gregory Bobish. Co-published simultaneously in *The Reference Librarian* (The Haworth Information Press, an imprint of The Haworth Press, Inc.) No. 77, 2002, pp. 71-88; and: *Distance Learning: Information Access and Services for Virtual Users* (ed: Hemalata Iyer) The Haworth Information Press, an imprint of The Haworth Press, Inc., 2002, pp. 71-88. Single or multiple copies of this article are available for a fee from The Haworth Document Delivery Service [1-800-HAWORTH, 9:00 a.m. - 5:00 p.m. (EST). E-mail address: getinfo@haworthpressinc.com].

INTRODUCTION

Over the last ten years, Internet use has increased significantly. Students are particularly eager to utilize this "convenient" medium to access materials for papers, projects, and assignments. Many students are opting to complete coursework off campus via distance education programs. Librarians are enthusiastic about using the Web to reach this audience for instructional purposes. They are rapidly creating library Web-based materials to teach students how to use online catalogs, databases, the Internet, and much more. Developers of library Web pages need to be thinking about accessibility issues, usability, and user-friendliness to create helpful materials.

INTERNET USAGE

Statistics show that in 1994, three million people were using the Internet. Within less than a decade, traffic on the information super highway grew exponentially. A study conducted by the Computer Industry Almanac, Inc. found that by the end of the year 2000, more than 400 million people worldwide were utilizing the Internet. Of these individuals, 130 million were from the United States. Estimates show that by 2005, five billion people could be accessing this electronic resource (*World Almanac and Book of Facts 2002*, 2002). In a study conducted by Alan L. Montgomery and Christos Faloutsos, findings showed that there was not only an increase in Internet use but that individual users were viewing more Web pages. "The median number of viewings per month in December 1999 was 310, more than twice the 150 viewings recorded in July 1997" (Montgomery, 2001). Internet user viewing time has also grown. "According to the National Science Foundation, the amount of time the average person spent on the Internet increased from fifteen hours per year in 1995 to 160 hours a year in 1999" (Schau, 2000). Using data collected from the supplement to the Current Population Survey, Schau found that the main uses of the Internet are for e-mail, searching for information, and checking the news. Additionally, "another popular use of the Internet was to take courses or do research for school. Thirty-six percent of those with Internet access at home used the Internet for such purposes" (Schau).

DISTANCE EDUCATION

The Internet is a wonderful delivery mechanism for distance education courses. Not surprisingly, distance education at postsecondary institutions is on the rise. A report issued by the National Education Association (NEA) presented findings from a national survey of distance education conducted by the National Center for Education Statistics (NCES). The NCES survey collected information about the 1997-1998 academic year. The report found that "the number of distance education courses offered was approximately double in 1997-98 what it was in 1994-95." An estimated 25,730 different distance education courses were offered in the 1994-95 academic year. This increased to 52,270 courses offered at any level, of which 47,540 were different college-level, credit-bearing courses. The NCES report indicated that in 1997-1998, most distance education providers used a variety of technologies to provide distance education instruction. These included Internet courses using asynchronous Web-based instruction, two-way interactive video, and one-way prerecorded video. The use of Internet-based instruction increased considerably between 1995 and 1997-98, nearly tripling "from twenty-two percent of institutions in 1995 to sixty percent of institutions in 1997-98" (Pena, 2000).

LITERATURE REVIEW

Web-based bibliographic instruction has been developed in response to several different needs. Both on- and off-campus students are eager to take advantage of the convenience and asynchronous nature of online resources. "Many students in college today accept Web use as the norm" (Dupuis, 1999). Librarians faced with dwindling resources and classroom time constraints have viewed online instruction as a way to reach more students than would be possible with traditional classroom-based instruction. The effectiveness of providing "point of need" instruction as opposed to a general instruction session has been debated in the literature (Herrington, 1998). In addition, many campuses have recently been faced with the challenge of meeting new information literacy requirements, and libraries have been major contributors to this effort (Dewald, 1999; Donaldson, 2000; Dupuis, 1999; Rosen, 2002). This additional instruction load makes the development of Web-based tools more intriguing.

The task of developing Web-based instruction materials has been approached in different ways, from providing electronic versions of existing print handouts and finding aids, to creating new, interactive tutorials which take fuller advantage of what Web technology has to offer. Collaboration with library and institutional systems departments can make this process much easier as well as insuring compatibility with system-wide infrastructure (Dewald, 1999; Dupuis, 2001; Smith, 2001). The content of these resources has expanded to include not only simple facts, but also more complicated concepts such as evaluation of sources, search strategies, and ethical use of information (Dewald, 1999; Donaldson, 2000; Dupuis, 1999; Germain et al., 2000). Critics of bibliographic instruction have suggested that librarians should focus on developing easier to use systems instead of on instruction programs to explain unnecessary complexities (Herrington, 1998), and while this may be true to some extent, it fails to address these more concept-based instructional needs.

One of the issues common to almost all online instruction projects is that of maintaining traditional bibliographic instruction ideals such as active and collaborative learning, concept-based teaching, and offering information in more than one medium. Web-based instruction lends itself well to interactive learning using frequent online questions/quizzes and the possibility of immediate feedback. Information literacy concepts and skills can be defined or discussed and then reinforced by exercises or assignments, especially if the instruction is course-related. Graphics and/or sound files provide a means of expressing a concept in different media to appeal to varied learning styles (Dewald, 1999; Donaldson, 2000; Germain et al., 2000).

When comparing traditional bibliographic instruction to online tutorials, it appears that there is no significant relationship between the format and the effectiveness of the tutorial in terms of improvement of users' research skills. In some specific cases, online tutorials were more successful in teaching the use of search strategies such as Boolean operators, probably due to the ease with which users could link directly from the tutorial to an actual database to try a search on their own. There was a general expectation that at least for now, online tutorials would be more effective in teaching mechanical skills and search strategies than in helping to convey more complicated evaluative skills, but the results of the studies did not clearly support this hypothesis (Germain et al., 2000; Holman, 2000).

A major advantage of online bibliographic instruction resources is the flexibility they offer both students and instructors. Self-paced tutorials offer students a sense of control that can add to their motivation and interest. Since an online lesson can be broken up into a number of modules, students can choose to complete one, several, or all of the modules in a session, depending on their specific needs (Dewald, 1999; Donaldson, 2000). Students can revisit an online instructional session, which is often not an alternative in traditional instruction (Germain et al., 2000).

Another way to offer flexibility as well as follow sound pedagogical technique is to provide students with an outline of the tutorial's educational objectives. This can be done through various means such as a table of contents, an index, or a site search engine, all of which can be hyper-linked to allow the student to jump to the part of the tutorial most useful for their purposes. Navigation options that allow users to return to a specific part of the tutorial are more user-friendly than a linear format that requires extensive use of browser buttons (Dewald, 1999).

Once the online instruction has been developed and put into use, evaluation and assessment are of the utmost importance to ensure that objectives are being met. The most immediate way of assessing learner satisfaction is through e-mail feedback options built into the tutorial itself. This allows users to voice concerns or ask questions as they arise and while not sufficient in and of itself, this does offer valuable insight into learners' reactions to the material. Course-related bibliographic instruction offers the most opportunity for feedback, as students can be given pre/post-tests to gauge improvement, assignments that require the use of skills taught by the tutorial, and formal evaluation forms. The librarian can also solicit feedback from the instructor of the class, who sees the result of the instruction in the students' subsequent work (Donaldson, 2000; Germain et al., 2000). Within the tutorial, quizzes can be offered after each module to provide reinforcement and feedback to the user as well as giving the instructor an idea of how well students are doing. If a satisfactory grade on the quiz is required to progress to the next part of the tutorial, a common base of knowledge can be assumed when developing the more advanced modules. However, this requires a bank of questions that can be randomly chosen for each quiz, so that a quiz can't be retaken and passed by simply guessing until the right answer is chosen (Rosen, 2002).

WEB PAGE DESIGN

Designing instructional Web pages requires a large commitment of time and energy. Be prepared to put in additional efforts for a project that in the long run will be fun, stimulating, and rewarding. Creating Web pages often entails learning new technologies and tapping into creative energies. Work with colleagues, students, and Webmasters to get input, guidance, and feedback. Whether you work one-on-one or brainstorm with numerous individuals, their assistance will be invaluable.

Building an instructional Web presence can be extremely beneficial for your library education program. Careful planning at the start of development will save on major adjustments in the long run. In the planning stages, short and long term goals should be drafted. This will provide a focus and help lay the groundwork for future endeavors. Your short-term goal may be to code a few "how to" guides within the coming year. However, your long-term goal is to have all of the "how to" guides mounted on the Internet. A page needs to be designed so that it can accommodate coming attractions, yet not look too sparse. Thoughtful planning will ensure that design layout enables smooth transformation from a small page to a larger site.

It is highly recommended to draft Web sites offline. As with computer programming, a blueprint of the design provides a frame of reference–it is often easy to get distracted and lose track of original intentions. The printed sketch, or storyboard, if it is an extensive project, should include goals and objectives and address content ideas, physical arrangement, technical issues, copyright, maintenance, usability, and evaluation criteria.

GOALS AND OBJECTIVES

Some preliminary questions need to be addressed before creating a Web page or tutorial. What is the purpose of the Web initiative? What do you want students to learn from using this Web resource? What message are you trying to get across? Who's in your audience?

At the University at Albany, a Web-based tutorial on evaluating Internet resources was created in 2001. It was developed because many students at the school were citing nonacademic Internet sites in assignments. The tutorial, located at http://library.albany.edu/usered/webeval/index.html, takes about fifteen to twenty minutes to complete. The goal and objectives of the instruction are on its lead page. The goal of this Web site is to help Internet users evaluate Internet Web pages. The objectives read as follows:

At the end of the virtual tutorial users will be able to:

- Evaluate Internet resources using the following criteria:

    Author
    Audience
    Scholarship
    Bias
    Currency
    Links

- Determine if the Web site meets your needs and standards of quality
- Apply what you have learned to evaluate all material, whether the format is electronic, print, non-print, etc.

By outlining the goals and objectives, users have an understanding of what the tutorial encompasses. This follows the same way librarians lay out their instruction plan at the beginning of an in-class session.

As with traditional instruction, it is imperative to know the intended audience of your Web site. If your aim is to reach students in their late teens or early twenties, your examples should be tailored to their interests. Undergraduates in this age range will relate to Snoop Dogg, Tool, or Britney Spears much more readily than Frank Sinatra, the Guess Who, or the Mothers of Invention. If your Web resources are being designed for a wider audience, try to include a variety of examples to capture the interest of as many users as possible.

CONTENT

The content of the instructional Web page is a priority. This is where the educational message is to be transmitted. Provide practical information that is applicable to students' coursework. Use vocabulary that users can understand. Your prose should flow so students can easily read it. Using jargon will make it difficult for users to comprehend your lesson. Librarians know the meaning of controlled vocabulary but many students do not. Don't overload them with extraneous material. Be cautious with taking printed handouts and mounting them on the Web. A guide that refers to resources located in the physical library may be hard to follow remotely. Read through all materials that are uploaded to the Internet for relevancy.

Text length is critical. Avoid being wordy. "It's more difficult to read from a computer screen than paper, strive for brevity" (Goldsborough, 2001). A study conducted by Jakob Nielsen and John Morkes showed that seventy-nine percent of Web users scan pages. They found the scan rate high because it takes twenty-five percent longer to read a computer screen than its print counterpart (Guglielmo, 1998). Better to link users to additional pages than bombard them with heavy sections of text. If lengthier passages are the only option include subheadings "that summarize key points" (Goldsborough, 2001).

PHYSICAL ARRANGEMENT

Structure the Web site so it is visually appealing and intuitive. Many students are savvy with navigating the Internet and will quickly link off your site if you do not grab their attention immediately. "You have 5-20 seconds (depending on who you believe) to capture your users' attention" (Fichter, 2001). Colors and fonts, graphics, hyperlinks, and layout are key requirements for creating an attractive and coherent Web page.

It may be very tempting to use flashy and bold colors, but be thoughtful. Loud and obnoxious Internet sites turn off many users. Web pages that are too light or have a dark or marbled background will be hard or impossible to read. These attributes will also cause printing problems unless the user is sophisticated enough to know how to change browser color preferences. Since this an instructional setting, it's best to be straightforward and uncomplicated. Colors and fonts provide an excellent avenue for continuity. The Web developer should use specific colors and fonts to highlight main ideas, subheadings, and important text.

The World Wide Web has many sites dedicated to color and font options. Projectcool Developerzone at http://www.projectcool.com/developer/reference/color-chart.html and Clearink's Palette Man at http://www.paletteman.com/ provide an array of colors. Palette Man has presets, which outline tones for tranquil, industrial, and refreshing moods. Larabie Fonts, at http://www.larabiefonts.com/fonts/c2.html, has a wide variety of font choices.

Graphics can really add pizzazz to a site and enhance instruction. Pictures, especially, can make the site and message more inviting. For example, a virtual tour that contains text details of the location of the reference desk, an accompanying map, and a picture of the staffed reference desk, will provide students with where to get reference help at the library.

http://library.albany.edu/usered/tour/ref/ref1.html

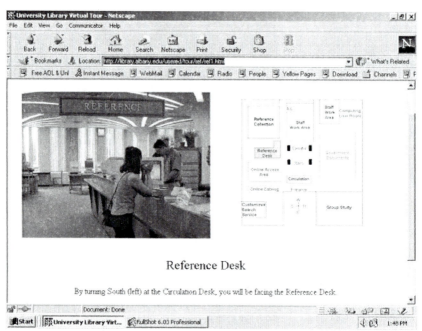

Reference Desk

By turning South (left) at the Circulation Desk, you will be facing the Reference Desk.

Photos of library staff helping patrons make your library more welcoming and may encourage users to come and search out your assistance and resources. They will be familiar with faces in the library and feel more comfortable when seeking guidance.

http://library.albany.edu/usered/tour/css/css2.html

University Library Virtual Tour

Our Customized Search
Service Provides:

- Searches on special
  databases
- Searches for people with
  disabilities
- Individualized instruction
- Search strategy consultation
- Citation searches for
  promotion / tenure
- Current awareness alerts

Image mapping can enhance graphics and text. Software such as Mapedit, available at http://www.boutell.com/mapedit/, makes it easy to transform a static image or passage into a "hot linked" resource. For example, you could teach students how to cite properly by utilizing this software. After scanning the title page of *Moby Dick*, Mapedit could be used to hotlink key citation elements (i.e., title, author, publisher, etc.) of the book. These elements would each be hyperlinked to an accurate citation of *Moby Dick* at its relevant counterpart (i.e., title to title, author to author). Students would be able to see where the placement of the title, author, etc., would be in an accurate citation. The image mapping application is perfect for virtual tours and call number location maps.

Graphics can be fun but you need to be cautious. An image that is very large may require a lot of load time. Most users want to breeze through a site and are impatient with time-consuming sites. "Slow downloading often lowers the level of trust the user has in the site and ultimately can cause lost traffic" (Joyce, 2001). If it is essential to include a high bit graphic, you may want to provide a thumbnail linked to the larger image, so students can get started on the page.

The two main file formats for graphics are JPEG (Joint Photographic Experts Group) and GIF (Graphic Interchange Format). GIFs have a limited 256-color palette and are best used with images with flat solid colors. JPEGs can contain up to 16,777,216 colors but their compression can have degradation of image quality. Photographs reproduce better as JPEGs (Descy, 1997).

Applets are also very appealing, but can be distracting. Noisy or blinking images may divert the student's attention from the instruction. Make sure all applets, graphics, and pictures relate to the instructional material. A fish swimming across the top of the Web site might look cool but it may confuse a student if the site is a guide to literary criticism.

Hyperlinks should also communicate a logical connection. Linking to external World Wide Web sites should be used sparingly. Studies show that URLs are volatile and page content may not remain constant (Koehler, 1999; Germain, 2000). Students will become frustrated with pulling up 404 Not Found error messages. Additionally, if every other word of the text is a hyperlink, main ideas get lost and users may link away from the page permanently.

The physical layout of a Web page should be undemanding and ordered. Utilize bullets, lists, and tables to organize materials in a logical fashion. "Using a familiar layout and site structure helps users. They expect the logo at the top, the content in the middle, menus on the left, and footers. Make use of their intuitive knowledge" (Fichter, 2001).

Be conservative with the number of screens you use. One or two screens of information are enough for the average user. "Research indicates that long Web pages (scrolling down the computer screen three or more pages) can cause a disorienting effect" (Ruffini, 2001).

Consistency is a prerequisite of any Web page. "The general look and feel of your pages should remain consistent. This assures students that they are still within your site" (Keating, 1999). If the site has a particular set of colors and fonts to track an idea or theme, continue to use those throughout the Web session. "Do not use the same icon as a metaphor for different concepts, or make the same type of icon clickable in one place but not in another" (Keating, 1999). Librarians strive to provide consistency within the classroom setting; this pattern should be duplicated in the electronic environment.

TECHNICAL ISSUES

When designing a Web site it is imperative to keep in mind: just because you can doesn't mean the user can. Your computer may be the top of the line model but don't assume that students will have identical equipment. Academic institutions own and have access to technology far more advanced than many of their users. High-bandwidth is a large issue especially for the remote individual. In the United States, only about six percent (or six million) households have high-bandwidth services (Moschella, 2001). You'll want to use technology that will work for your users. "The last thing a provider of online learning wants is to have a client in a remote or overseas location unable to access a module that has been paid for, because they have an incompatible browser or unreliable connection. This is a problem that should be overcome by responsible use of technology during the design stages" (McCann, 2002).

Avoid using plug-ins, large graphics and applets, or anything that requires additional software to upload. Though many software packages are free and can be linked and easily uploaded from your Web site, many users will avoid these pages. This entails extra work and many users are uncomfortable with certain technologies and feel intimidated. Keep in mind the mission of the Web site is to teach library instruction, not software instruction.

COPYRIGHT

The World Wide Web is provocative because so many resources are available for free. Or so it seems. It is very easy to click on the right mouse button and download an image onto your Web site, but beware. Copyright law protects many images found on the Internet; don't assume fair use just because a search engine was able to locate and display it (Tomaiuolo, 2002). Ask Web site owners for permission for all material, including text, images, audio, video, applets, and banners. Even though government sites are public domain, it is polite to ask for consent.

Be considerate with linking to someone else's pages and/or content. Your site might generate more users than a Web builder's server can handle. Again, here is a situation where it's best to ask the site owner for access authorization. New technologies such as digital cameras and Photoshop make it easy to generate your own artwork, trouble free of copyright headaches.

MAINTENANCE

Web-based resources require continuous monitoring and maintenance. Problems that arise and need to be addressed include inactive hyperlinks, content changes, and technological modifications. Try to use examples you create and store on internal files. Host the content of other pages (e.g., government documents, public domain information) on your server. This will avoid dead links if the site is taken down. Problems also surface with content changes. At the University at Albany, a Web tutorial was designed to teach students how to use the online catalog. Screen shots were used as examples. When the catalog was upgraded the tutorial needed to be updated. In the planning stage of a Web tutorial, changes in technology resources need to be researched. Using a generic strategy also saves on maintenance difficulties. This will teach students basic library concepts rather than institutional or vendor related services and products.

USABILITY

Testing Web pages for accuracy, understandability, and technical errors is critical. Use Web analysis tools, such as Doctor HTML at http://www2.imagiware.com/RxHTML/ or Web Site Garage at http://www.websitegarage.com. These review Web pages for coding, spelling, and other errors and produce detailed reports.

Make sure Web pages are accessible to individuals with disabilities. Include text alternatives to audio, videos, and other images. Follow the W3C guidelines to make a Web site that is inviting to all (Smith, 2001). Bobby, at http://www.cast.org/bobby, analyzes Web pages to ensure accessibility (Vind, 2000).

Recruit fellow colleagues, students, and staff to review your work. There are never too many people to evaluate an instructional Web page. It is much better to have spelling, grammar, content, and visual errors discovered before the page goes "live" than to be embarrassed publicly. Take all feedback seriously. What may seem like an easy concept for a librarian may be very tricky for a student to comprehend. Students in particular provide wonderful insight into your Web tools. You may want to develop a short questionnaire to make sure main ideas were conveyed.

A winning Web site is a usable Web site. "To be successful at user-focused design, be observant. Watch users every chance you get and think about their behaviors and performances" (Fitcher, 2001). By observing, you can see if users are navigating the site for its designed intention. If your site requires students to enter data, include utilities that capture this information and analyze the records. A Web site designed as a library term glossary is ineffective if students are entering topic words or phrases in the search window instead of library-oriented vocabulary. They might be thinking your site is the online catalog, a database, or a search engine. Simple modifications can make the purpose of the site unambiguous.

Web pages should also be tested in different browsers and on different machines. A Web site loaded onto Netscape 6.0 may look spectacular but may look awful on Explorer, and vice versa. Also, check for load time of images and bit-consuming gadgets. If you expect students to print out your materials, test this out. Information within a frame or on specific software, such as Adobe Acrobat, may be difficult or impossible to print.

EVALUATION

Use of Web instructional tools requires a different evaluation strategy than is traditionally used in library classroom instruction. Person-to-person instruction allows the librarian to quickly summarize if a student is grasping the material presented. Visual cues such as frantically waving hands and glazed over eyes are lost. Remote instruction, where no visual interaction transpires, makes evaluation trickier. Carefully crafted Web tutorials can incorporate mechanisms to determine if the presented material is understood. Within the interactive tutorials created at the University at Albany Libraries, Web pages contain multiple-choice questions with radio buttons. Once students submit the form, correct answers are displayed with explanations. Data from the electronic forms are collected and reviewed by librarians to assess instruction effectiveness. The tutorial covering the Libraries' online catalog, search strategies, and a database contains a page where students have the option to submit questions. Answers are processed and directly e-mailed to students within forty-eight hours.

http://library.albany.edu/usered/tut/pag20.html

Feedback is also collected from answers submitted to credit pages. These pages were created in response to professors requiring completion of tutorials as assignments. Students enter their name, e-mail, course information, and comments and/or questions.

http://library.albany.edu/usered/webeval/credit.html

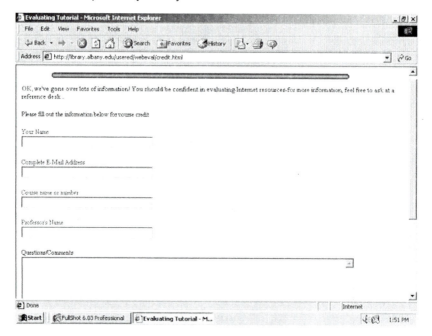

As follows is a sample of student submissions:

"Some of the Websites were funny."

"The step by step tour makes me feel more comfortable with going to the library instead of feeling overwhelmed when I walk in."

"This tutorial was a good reminder of what's important without dragging it out."

"I have officially had 10 minutes of my life, robbed. Thank you."

"Very helpful, good assignment."

"I'm actually [sic] doing a report right now that consists a lot of online sites as my research, after doing this I will now look more closely at each page before getting my information from it."

Reactions from the tutorials have provided the library with a wealth of information about students and what they think about the library, its services, and resources. Many of the virtual tour replies pointed to students feeling "overwhelmed" or "intimidated" by the University Library, which is a large research-oriented library. The tour familiarizes students with the library so they are more comfortable when coming into the physical building. Now that we know how anxious students are with the University Library, we can address making the library more engaging.

These comments also let Web developers know students' feelings about the Web-based instruction. Overwhelmingly, responses have been positive, with students reporting that the tutorials were "helpful," "interesting," and "enjoyable." Of course, there are students who are bored or not interested, but that cannot be avoided in any instructional format. Some users provide suggestions about content or layout. This feedback is reviewed and pages are modified if it is felt that changes will be helpful and make the tutorial more useful.

TILT–A MODEL INTERACTIVE WEB-BASED TUTORIAL

The Texas Information Literacy Tutorial (TILT) found at http://tilt.lib.utsystem.edu/ is an outstanding example of what online tutorials can achieve when sufficient resources and opportunities for collaboration are available. This tutorial was developed at the University of Texas at Austin in response to the implementation of a campus-wide information literacy program. In order to serve the greatest number of undergraduates at the University, the project development team decided to develop a "web-based tutorial that could be integrated into a variety of first-year courses" (Dupuis, 2001). In creating the tutorial, the three major people responsible collaborated with a wide variety of specialists including programmers, representatives of the systems department, and artists who designed the graphics on the site. There was also substantial consultation with faculty from numerous departments to ensure the widest possible application of the tutorial.

The tutorial is composed of an "introduction to dispel some common misconceptions about the Internet" and three modules covering different aspects of the research process. Students can work at their own pace as well as having the opportunity to "select one of six 'Internet issues' that most interest them: censorship, business, law, security, trends, and global communities" (Dupuis, 2001). The issue students choose is then highlighted as they work their way through the modules, heightening interest and motivation.

TILT's creators emphasize that the tutorial is intended as "a supplement to library instruction, not a replacement" (Dupuis, 2001). Students who complete the tutorial are recognized as having an information literacy foundation, and then can work on more complex topics discussed in traditional classroom settings.

Originally designed for the use of University of Texas students, TILT aroused widespread interest among the bibliographic instruction community. The creators of the tutorial have generously allowed linking permission to outside users. Librarians and instructors can use the Website for their classes or libraries. Students anywhere can register as a TILT user and take the quizzes at the end of each module. Their test results are then e-mailed to their instructor where they can be included as part of a class grade or given as an extra credit assignment.

Most recently, TILT has become available in a downloadable version, complete with scripts and documentation, called "yourTILT." This version of the tutorial is available free of charge under an Open Publication License (OPL), which allows anyone to alter or add to the tutorial as long as the resulting tutorial is made available under an OPL. This enables educators to customize the tutorial for their institution or to add subject specific sections. Though the time invested in developing this tutorial was enormous (two to eight hours per day, plus some weekends, for at least one and a half years) the pedagogical outcome is extensive. The success and widespread use of TILT indicate that sharing resources can be extremely beneficial both for librarians, and perhaps most importantly, the students they serve.

WEB CODING TOOLS

Many of the Web sites previously mentioned were created using a variety of Web development tools. Developers can hand-code HTML in packages like Notepad or Wordpad. Others author using software, such as Dreamweaver, which for many can be complicated. Products using either application are viewable on most browsers including Netscape, Explorer, or Opera. Adding JavaScripts to a site can make static pages more engaging with generated messages such as quotes, definitions, or highlights of the day. *Javascripts.com* has over 7,000 scripts that can be copied and pasted, provided the script author is credited.

New scripting languages such as PHP (Hypertext Preprocessor) offer tutorial developers the ability to dynamically alter tutorial navigation (Abualsamid, 2000). The program responds to user input and traverses accordingly. If a user is consistently having difficulty answering certain questions, the program will automatically redirect users to section(s) of the tutorial that review troublesome concepts. Instructors can monitor students' progress through the different modules. Users are authenticated with a username and password, allowing librarians the ability to assess student navigation patterns and determine problems and successes.

Streaming media, which include video, audio, and other multimedia applications, allow users to play files without waiting for complete download (Smith, 2001). As the patron is watching the beginning of the video, the rest of the file is downloading in the background. Since most video files are relatively large, download time may be longer than actual viewing time. Streaming is an excellent way to offer video-based instruction to patrons without broadband Web access.

CONCLUSION

These innovative technologies have made it possible to develop and deliver library instruction in a very exciting venue. New networked utilities have presented novel approaches to teaching students about library resources and services. Distance learners and remote users can now learn in a preferred setting and at a favored time. Librarians can reach students who were once extremely inaccessible, as well as learners who are partial to computer-based resources. Many of these individuals find Internet instruction more interesting and enjoyable. Supplementing traditional in-class sessions with Web-based assignments will assist librarians in providing a more rounded academic experience to college constituents.

The design of library-based Web instruction requires the use of the same pedagogical practices utilized in live classroom settings. As educators, librarians need to continue to focus on: teaching specific library concepts in Web sessions; adapting these tools for appropriate audiences; appraising student outcomes; assessing usability; and modifying tools to maintain a superior learning environment.

REFERENCES

Abualsamid, A. (2000, September 24). PHP language serves up Web apps. *Electronic Engineering Times*, 1129, 94-95.

Computers and the Internet (2002). In *World Almanac and Book of Facts 2002* (pp. 628-629). New York: World Almanac Books.

Descy, D. E. (1997). All aboard the Internet: Web page design, part II. *Techtrends*, 42 (2), 3-5.

Dewald, N. (1999). Web-Based Library Instruction: What Is Good Pedagogy? *Information Technology and Libraries*, 18 (1), 26-31.

Dewald, N. (1999). Transporting Good Library Instruction Practices into the Web Environment: An Analysis of Online Tutorials. *The Journal of Academic Librarianship*, 25 (1), 26-32.

Donaldson, K. (2000). Library Research Success: Designing An Online Tutorial to Teach Information Literacy Skills to First-Year Students. *The Internet and Higher Education*, 2 (4), 237-251.

Dupuis, E. (2001). Automating Instruction. *Library Journal* (Suppl.), 21-22.

Dupuis, E. (1999). The creative evolution of library instruction. *Reference Services Review*, 27 (3), 287-290.

Fichter, D. (2001). Designing usable sites: A state of mind. *Online*, 25 (1), 68-70.

Germain C. (2000). URLs: Uniform resource locators or unreliable resource locators. *College & Research Libraries*, 61 (4), 359-65.

Germain, C., Jacobson, T. (2000). A comparison of the effectiveness of presentation formats for instruction: teaching first year students at SUNY Albany. *College and Research Libraries*, 61 (1), 65-72.

Guglielmo, C. (1998). Sun sheds light on site-building for success. *Inter@ctive*, 5 (1), 35.

Goldsborough, R. (2001). Weaving web sites that others will want to use. *Community College Week*, 13 (13), 17.

Herrington, V. (1998). Way beyond BI: A look to the future. *Journal of Academic Librarianship*, 24 (5), 381-386.

Holman, L. (2000). A Comparison of Computer-Assisted Instruction and Classroom Bibliographic Instruction. *Reference & User Services Quarterly*, 40 (1), 53-60.

Joyce, B. (2001). The print-to-web evolution and the importance of usability. *Public Roads*, 65 (3), 56.

Keating, A. B. & Hargitai, J. (1999). *The wired professor: A guide to incorporating the World Wide Web in college instruction*. New York: New York University Press.

Koehler, W. (1999). An analysis of web page and web site constancy and permanence. *Journal of the American Society of Information Science*, 50 (2), 162-180.

McCann, D. & Mead, N. (2002). A case study in the usability of e-learning. *Journal of Banking and Financial Services*, 116 (1), 44-46.

Montgomery, A. L. & Faloutsos, C. (2001). Identifying web browsing trends and patterns. *Computer*, 34 (7), 94-95.

Moschella, D. (2001). Feds must widen the on-ramp for high bandwidth. *Computerworld*, 35 (22), 27.

Pena, D. & Maitland, C. (2000). *Distance Education at Postsecondary Education Institutions: 1997-98* NEA Higher Education Research Center Update v6 n2 Apr 2000 (ERIC Document Reproduction Service No. ED455 754).

Rosen, J. & Castro, G. (2002). From workbook to Web: Building an information literacy oasis. *Computers in Libraries*, 22 (1), 30-35.

Ruffini, M. F. (2001). Blueprint to develop a great web site. *T H E Journal*, 28 (8), 64-70.

Schau, T. (2000). "Internet use: Here, there and everywhere." *Occupational Outlook Quarterly*, 44 (4), 40-47.

Smith, S. S. (2001). *Web-Based Instruction: A Guide for Libraries*. Chicago: American Library Association.

Tomaiuolo, N. G. (2002).When image is everything: Finding and using graphics from the Web. *Searcher*, 10 (1), 10-20.

Vind, O. (2000). Make your web site healthier with HTML code Checkup. *Computers in Libraries*, 20 (1), 40-43.

Information Literacy
at Ulster County Community College:
Going the Distance

Robin Walsh

SUMMARY. In 1996, the reference librarians and faculty at Ulster County Community College developed an award-winning online information literacy course. The course is now offered through the SUNY Learning Network and is part of the OASIS distance education program at UCCC. LIB111 evolved through an extensive information literacy initiative starting in 1992 and is based on the 1-credit classroom course that had been taught at UCCC since 1994. It is a pre/co-requisite for all second semester English courses. Faculty development and maintenance of the course are continuing responsibilities. Retention and assessment are issues that are now being addressed. *[Article copies available for a fee from The Haworth Document Delivery Service: 1-800-HAWORTH. E-mail address: <getinfo@haworthpressinc.com> Website: <http://www.HaworthPress.com> © 2002 by The Haworth Press, Inc. All rights reserved.]*

KEYWORDS. Distance learning, SUNY Learning Network, faculty development, virtual reference services

Robin Walsh is Librarian, Macdonald DeWitt Library, Ulster County Community College, Stone Ridge, NY 12484 (E-mail: walshr@sunyulster.edu).

[Haworth co-indexing entry note]: "Information Literacy at Ulster County Community College: Going the Distance." Walsh, Robin. Co-published simultaneously in *The Reference Librarian* (The Haworth Information Press, an imprint of The Haworth Press, Inc.) No. 77, 2002, pp. 89-105; and: *Distance Learning: Information Access and Services for Virtual Users* (ed: Hemalata Iyer) The Haworth Information Press, an imprint of The Haworth Press, Inc., 2002, pp. 89-105. Single or multiple copies of this article are available for a fee from The Haworth Document Delivery Service [1-800-HAWORTH, 9:00 a.m. - 5:00 p.m. (EST). E-mail address: getinfo@haworthpressinc.com].

INTRODUCTION

Ulster County Community College, a unit of the State University of New York (SUNY), is located in Stone Ridge, close to the geographic center of Ulster County in the Hudson River Valley. The main campus consists of 165 acres of sloping meadowland and apple orchards and offers views of the Catskill Mountains to the west and the Shawangunks to the east. Fall enrollment is typically around 2,700 students. The student population is diverse. About 1/3 of the students are traditionally aged recent high school graduates and high school students who participate in a "bridge" program. The student body includes single parents, retired persons, students with disabilities and people from business and industry. Many are returning to the classroom after an absence of ten or more years. The students are almost evenly divided between full and part-time, 60% female and 91% white.

There are currently 64 full-time faculty members and approximately 130 adjunct instructors at Ulster County Community College. The college offers almost 600 credit bearing courses and has conferred over 14,000 degrees since it was founded in 1962.

DISTANCE LEARNING AT UCCC

Ulster County Community College offers a fully accredited online A.S. Degree in individual Studies through the SUNY Learning Network (SLN). The flexibility of the program allows students to select courses that meet their educational and professional goals. Course selections must, of course, be applicable to the degree program and be approved by the student's academic adviser at UCCC. Students may select from over 300 courses offered by the many SUNY colleges and universities that make up the Learning Network. Of the 300 courses offered by SLN, 26 classes are being offered this semester (Spring 2002) by UCCC and seven of those are information literacy. All of these courses are taught on the Web and require the student to have access to a personal computer with access to the Internet.

The Individual Studies Program at UCCC combines courses in natural science, humanities, and social sciences with a series of classes that are selected to fulfill individual goals. In addition to the convenience of taking courses from a home or office computer, the UCCC OASIS program also allows a student to transfer as many as 30 credits to Ulster from other accredited institutions. These credits may be either online courses or traditional credit courses.

Information about the OASIS program is available at the Ulster County Community College Web site at <http://www.sunyulster.edu/programs/oasis. asp>.

INFORMATION LITERACY AT UCCC

In 1992, instruction librarian Patricia Carroll-Mathes and the Macdonald DeWitt Library's new director, Larry Berk, began an Information Literacy Initiative at UCCC. There were no other community colleges in New York State for them to emulate. In 1992 Library Orientation Exchange (LOEX) reported undergraduate for-credit library instruction courses being offered at only four colleges: Montgomery College, Iona College, The University of New Mexico, and The University of Oklahoma.

That the information literacy course at UCCC should be credit bearing was one of the decisions that was made early in the development process. Kimberley M. Donnelly describes four approaches to library instruction (Donnelly 47):

1. The Course-Integrated Model. Faculty members, with assistance from reference librarians, address research with their students in the context of class instruction and specific assignments. In this model, subject librarians usually work with teaching faculty to integrate information literacy into all classroom instruction.
2. The Elective, For-Credit Course Model. A small percentage of the students at a college are offered an information literacy elective. Specific programs may require the course but, overall, it is optional.
3. The Required, Discipline-Specific, For-Credit Course Model assumes that students are more motivated to learn if library instruction is offered in discipline specific research tools related to particular courses. It differs from the Elective Model only in that it is required.
4. The Required, Core-Curriculum For-Credit Model assumes that there is a certain level of competency that all students should achieve regardless of their major.

The fourth model presented by Donnelly is the model adopted at Ulster County Community College. In fact, these four approaches are not mutually exclusive. The goal at UCCC is that the course-integrated model will run parallel to LIB111 (Berk and Mathes 83).

The library would also involve faculty in the information literacy course from its conception, through the development and into the implementation of the course. To offer a credit-bearing information literacy course involving faculty as instructors made this particular project unique at a time when many other libraries were still trying to meet Association of College and Research Library (ACRL) Information Literacy Standards for Higher Education by giving freshmen a 20-minute tour of the library.

Pat Carroll-Mathes and Larry Berk had already surveyed what was being done at other colleges through contact with other libraries, professional organizations and LOEX Clearinghouse. They had also identified some of the influential members of the faculty who would have to back any successful effort, and engaged in a lobbying effort to gain their support. Patricia Carroll-Mathes had recently returned from a sabbatical during which she had attended LOEX and the Workshop on Instruction in Library Use (WILU). She used her required sabbatical report to the board of trustees and the faculty to define information literacy and the course that the library hoped to offer. Pursuing the idea of offering a for-credit course, Pat Carroll-Mathes and Larry Berk proposed and gained approval of a two-credit elective course similar to those being offered at several other 4-year colleges.

But even as the curriculum committee was approving the course, it became clear that there were several problems with a two-credit course. Many programs at the college were already at their upper limit for required courses. Those programs would not consider a two-credit course as an added requirement. If the course were going to become a requirement, it would have to be 1-credit. It was also clear that there were not enough librarians employed at Macdonald DeWitt Library to teach several sections of a two-credit course. The college was unwilling and unable to hire more librarians. Existing faculty would have to be trained to teach the course. For some reason this idea—that the library should use faculty to teach—has been what librarians at other colleges deem to be UCCC's most radical decision.

In 1993 the two-credit information literacy course spawned both a one-credit course and a three-credit course. The three-credit course was popular when it was introduced, at least with older students and independent scholars in the community, but the one-credit course became the focus of the library's efforts.

There was some resistance to the introduction of the new Information Literacy courses because faculty had barely begun to use or understand the library's electronic resources and didn't see the need for a course in information literacy. They did not expect research resources to change as quickly as they were changing and believed that students would "just know" how to use them. The Academic Dean and the Teaching/Learning Center sponsored two training sessions for faculty and staff. At the least, training sessions would make faculty aware of the library's resources and more of those resources might be incorporated into existing courses. The training sessions would also serve as the first step toward the library's goal of recruiting faculty to teach the Information Literacy course. A joint letter sent to both full-time and adjunct faculty was followed by personal contacts and persistent follow-up. The two eight-hour training sessions were developed and taught by three librarians over four days. The textbook was *Introduction to Information Research* by Carla List. When those first training sessions were over, 36% of the full-time faculty, 5% of the part-time faculty and 15% of the professional staff had completed the training.

Subsequent faculty development sessions have been funded by a Title III grant. This has allowed the college to offer an honorarium to faculty for attending the course. Staff is also welcome to attend.

Library Director Larry Berk taught the first section of the one-credit LIB111 course in the spring of 1995. The director of the Teaching/Learning Center, chemistry professor Dennis Swauger, was the first faculty member to teach a section in the fall of 1995. By the following semester, three more faculty members had joined him in teaching the course. Patricia Carroll-Mathes acted as coordinator and offered to team teach with faculty and support them in other ways. A special section of LIB111 was later offered for the librarians in the Kingston City School District, and it was through this course that the library hired Tamara Katzowitz, now a long-time instructor at the Business Resource Center in Kingston, NY.

In 1996 the groundwork and lobbying efforts paid off when the Chemical Dependency and Human Services Departments adopted the one-credit information literacy course, offered as LIB111, as a program requirement. Shortly after that, the Nursing and Business Departments also adopted it as a requirement.

While LIB111 was still being developed as a classroom course at UCCC, activities that would affect the online course were already underway, though no one knew it at the time. In collaboration with Southeastern New York Library Resources Council (SENYLRC), UCCC developed a "train the trainers" course funded by an LSCA grant. Three fifteen-hour sessions were offered to school, public and academic librarians who would return to their libraries and offer training sessions. Thirty-four librarians from SENYLRC's eight-county region took the training. Down the road, several of them have taught LIB111 at UCCC in the classroom and online.

LIB111 GOES ON THE WWW

In 1996 Macdonald DeWitt Library received a grant from SUNY Office of Educational Technology to redesign the one-credit classroom information literacy course for online delivery on the WWW. A development team made up of both librarians and faculty was formed, consisting of: Honey Fein, Professor Emerita Nursing; Patricia Carroll-Mathes, Coordinator of Information Literacy; Larry Berk, Director of Library & Information Services; Ed Peifer, Professor of Mathematics; Cheri Gerstung, Head of Reference; and Kathleen Bruegging, Professor of Foreign Languages.

The chair of the content development team, Honey Fein, was also the chair of the UCCC Nursing Department. She had been a strong supporter of the information literacy course from the very beginning and the course would not exist without her and other faculty like her. Before joining the development team, Honey had taken the information literacy training offered through the UCCC Teaching/Learning Center, and audited Larry Berk's spring 1995 section of the course before teaching the course herself with the library's team-teaching support.

Putting LIB111 online was, once again, a collaborative effort. Librarians and faculty at UCCC worked together and consulted with librarians and faculty at several other SUNY institutions, in particular, the School of Education at SUNY Albany.

The team identified priorities. They wanted the course to be interactive. They wanted to engage students in hands-on activities. They wanted the design of the course to be flexible and to accommodate changes in electronic tools. They also wanted the course to be technically accessible to students who, typically, do not buy a new computer every year. The course was designed to introduce students to the organization, retrieval and evaluation of electronic and print information. Students are provided with an overview of college library systems, networked information systems, traditional scholarly resources, evolving delivery systems, and the concepts underlying the research process. The course addresses the changing nature of information delivery rather than the use of one specific research tool. To complete the assignments, students use print resources, electronic databases, and the World Wide Web. Exercises lead students through thinking critically when formulating research queries and evaluating books, journal articles and Web sites. The design team later decided to add a lesson to the course that would discuss intellectual property rights, academic honesty and the proper use of citation.

It was also in 1996 that Patricia Carroll-Mathes was the recipient of the Innovation in Instruction Award from the Instruction Section of the Association of College and Research Libraries (ACRL) for the Collaborative Information Literacy Project. The Awards Committee praised the UCCC Information Literacy Project as being both exciting and innovative when they honored her at their annual dinner in New York City.

LIB111 was offered online through the SUNY Learning Network (SLN) for the first time in the fall of 1997. The SLN is a State University of New York program that supports SUNY campuses working collaboratively to offer distance learning courses and degree programs. The SLN is sponsored by Advanced Learning & Information Services, which is part of the Office of the Provost at SUNY System Administration. It is important to note that SLN is not another degree granting institution and not part of any individual campus.

SLN is designed to provide services that each individual campus would otherwise have to create or reinvent on its own. There is also a variety of support resources to assist a faculty member developing a course for the SUNY Learning Network. SLN provides a course template in Lotus Notes™. The template is designed to be asynchronous so that, while learning is both interactive with faculty and collaborative with classmates, students are not required to be at a certain place at a certain time and a variety of schedules can be accommodated. The template also allows some flexibility of level of interaction with other students in the class. Students submit material that will be seen by other students when they introduce themselves, post announcements on the bulletin board, or when they choose the option to allow other students to read their posting. Students may submit assignments that may be read only by themselves and the instructor. Students even have a private folder to save their work where no one else can see it.

Faculty who taught LIB111 online received training both at UCCC and from SLN. In 1996 Dennis Swauger taught one online section of LIB111 exclusively for UCCC faculty. Those instructors also met in the classroom with Dennis and Patricia Carroll-Mathes to discuss teaching issues. Faculty who then decided to teach the online course received three days of training from SLN that addressed both instructional design issues and Lotus Notes™.

In 1997 and 1998, LIB111 was taught to students both in the classroom and online, with both librarians and faculty as instructors. In 1998 LIB111 became, virtually, a required course when it was adopted by the English Department as a co/pre-requisite to second semester English courses ENG102 and ENG227.

The next major opportunity for Macdonald DeWitt Library came in 1999, when the State University of New York (SUNY) Office of Library and Information Services (OLIS) Information Literacy Web-Based Task Force produced an RFP for a Web-based information literacy course. On completion, the course would be made available to all SUNY libraries at no charge.

The roots of this RFP actually went back to 1996 when the SUNY Council of Library Directors (SCLD) appointed an Information Literacy Committee and charged the committee with identifying desired information literacy competencies across the curriculum, and with developing a process to implement a SUNY-wide information literacy initiative in SUNY institutions.

The Final Report of the Committee was submitted on September 30, 1997, and called for the involvement of OLIS in developing funding for a SUNY-wide initiative for implementing a distance learning information literacy course. The SUNY Information Literacy Initiative Task Force, chaired by Maryruth Glogowski, felt strongly that information literacy competencies needed to be identified prior to content development. The committee specified the following nine competencies:

1. To recognize the need for information.
2. To access information from appropriate sources.
3. To develop skills in using information technologies.
4. To critically analyze and evaluate information.
5. To organize and process information.

6. To apply information for effective and creative decision making.
7. To generate and effectively communicate information and knowledge.
8. To understand and respect the ethical, legal, and socio-political aspects of information and its technologies.
9. To develop attitudinal objectives that lead to appreciation of lifelong learning.

To follow up on this report, SCLD appointed a SUNY Information Literacy Web-based Task Force in 1997. The principal charge to this group was to develop or adopt a modular, generic Web-based information literacy course for use throughout the SUNY system. The Final Report of this group was submitted on April 24, 1998. The Task Force did not develop or adopt an information literacy course but did offer the following nine modules as a suggested outline for the creation of a course:

Module 1: Introduction to Information

Module 2: Formulating a Research Question

Module 3: Developing Effective Search Strategies

Module 4: Basic Information Resources in Various Formats

Module 5: Electronic Library Catalogs (Online public access catalogs)

Module 6: Indexes and Abstracts: How They Work

Module 7: Searching the World Wide Web Effectively for Information

Module 8: Evaluating the Information You Find

Module 9: Recording Your Information

At this point, the SUNY Office of Library & Information Services stepped in with funding that would allow the creation of a generic Web-based information literacy course. They limited the proposal process to the SUNY community.

On April 27, 1999, OLIS released RFP for Web-based course template to be made available to all SUNY institutions (http://www.sunyconnect.suny.edu/ili/ILRFP.doc). The specific requirements described in the RFP were selected with considerable help from members of the SUNYLA Library Instruction Committee.

In short, the RFP specified that the successful proposer would create and deliver a Web-based course that will provide a general introduction to information literacy. The course developed would be written in simple HTML and will otherwise be platform independent. The course would address itself to generic information literacy competencies and would not address discipline specific competencies. Individual libraries adopting the course would be able to modify it to specific local needs. The course would also address itself to information in a range of formats, including print, non-print and electronic (online or CD-ROM). The course would also provide a glossary or other convenient means of accessing brief definitions or explanations of key terms and concepts. Complicated or extensive graphics were not required by the RFP and were to be in the public domain, used by permission, or created for the course.

An evaluation team representing SUNY librarians, the SUNY Learning Network, SUNY education faculty, and OLIS reviewed the proposals that were submitted in response to the RFP.

On August 5, 1999, the SUNY Office of Library & Information Services announced the selection of Ulster County Community College to develop the Web-based information literacy course for the SUNY System. The team unanimously recommended the Ulster proposal to Carey Hatch, Assistant Provost for Library & Information Services, who concurred. The completed course would be due to be submitted for acceptance testing in spring of 2000. After acceptance, OLIS intended to make the course available for use throughout SUNY.

In October, 1999 the design team that had created the online course at UCCC in 1996 regrouped to review the existing course and determine how much of it could be re-used in the course that would be submitted to OLIS. By this time, Patricia Carroll-Mathes had retired from her position at UCCC. New team members included: Ruth Boetcker, Interim Coordinator of Information Literacy; Kari Mack, Associate Director; and Lou Skaar, Chair of the English Department. CollegisEduprise, a contractor that provides UCCC technical support, supplied some instructional design and technical recommendations.

The course was reviewed first by the entire UCCC team and then by the instructional designer from CollegisEduprise, and by the Office of Information Technology executive and technical directors. Student aides working in the Macdonald DeWitt Library acted as guinea pigs to test the revised course. At the time that the course was being developed, OLIS did not require ADA compliance, but the course was tested using JAWS for Windows and for use on the Kurzweil Omni 3000.

The redesigned Information Literacy course ended up with an introduction and four modules that corresponded, in content but not in number, with the modules recommended by the SUNY Council of Library Directors Information Literacy Committee in 1997.

Introduction
    The Information Age
Module 1 Searching Databases
    Lesson 1–What is a Database?
    Lesson 2–Indexing and Searching
    Lesson 3–The Search Process
    Lesson 4–Evaluation of Information
    Lesson 5–Citation of Source(s) Used
Module 2 Searching for Library Materials
    Lesson 1–Using Classification and Access Systems
    Lesson 2–Using WorldCat and FirstSearch
Module 3 Searching for Reference Sources–Print and Electronic
    Lesson 1–Role of Reference Sources/Tools in the Research Process
    Lesson 2–Encyclopedias and Atlases
    Lesson 3–Book Reviews
    Lesson 4–Periodical Indices and Abstracts
    Lesson 5–Miscellaneous Resources
Module 4 Searching the Internet
    Lesson 1–Using the Internet
    Lesson 2–Web Directories
    Lesson 3–Search Engines
    Lesson 4–Legal & Socio-Political Aspects of Information

In April 2000 UCCC submitted the redesigned information literacy course to OLIS. Two months later the course was accepted and made available to all SUNY colleges for downloading from the OLIS Web site.

The course that was accepted by OLIS differs considerably from LIB111 as it is offered by UCCC through SLN. LIB111 begins with considerable introductory material including contact information and a syllabus. There are opening activities so that the teacher and students may introduce themselves. There are assignments that accompany each module and a final exam. When the last module has been completed, students are asked to complete a survey. The course, as it is available from OLIS, consists of only the introduction and four modules. SUNY campuses can choose to mount any or all of the four modules locally and modify them for use as a tutorial or in their own information literacy teaching programs.

Nearly every SUNY campus has downloaded the course to look at it. Some have decided to adapt all or some of the modules as part of their own information literacy courses. For example, Milne Library at SUNY Oneonta has adapted the modules downloaded from OLIS as a supplementary tutorial to their course INTD 150: Library & Internet Research.

There is a link from their Information Literacy and Instruction Web page at <http://www.oneonta.edu/library/infoliteracy/infolit.html>.

Melvil Dewey Library and Media Center at Jefferson Community College is using the modules as an online tutorial for their students. This tutorial is available at <http://www.sunyjefferson.edu/Library/libmjp.html>. SUNY Oneonta is using it as a supplementary tutorial to their course INTD 150: Library & Internet Research. The Science and Engineering Web page at Duke University Libraries also links to the course modules. OLIS has received a number of inquiries from colleges outside of SUNY who are interested in using the course.

From time to time librarians at other colleges will contact UCCC to say that they are in the process of developing an information literacy course or that they have developed one but that their faculty or administration has not accepted it. They ask what happened here at UCCC to make the course accepted by the administration and the faculty. They are almost never completely satisfied with the answers that we are able to give them. There was no secret to making LIB111 successful and there was no magic moment when it happened. The success of LIB111 came as a result of the persistent work of people in the library. Larry Berk and Patricia Carroll-Mathes met with administrators and faculty, face to face, over and over again, until the key people on campus were convinced that information literacy was a priority. We can sympathize with librarians who have been given the charge of coming up with a successful information literacy course by next semester, but we have no magic to offer them. Work on LIB111 started in 1992; it was not accepted as a program requirement by the first academic department until 1996 and did not go online until 1997.

Fortunately, other librarians need not start at the beginning where UCCC started. The course modules for LIB111 are available free to any SUNY college from OLIS. There are also many other alternatives developed more recently, including the winner of the ACRL Instruction Section Innovation in Instruction Award in the year 2000, Texas Information Literacy Tutorial (TILT). TILT is available via an Open Publication License (OPL), free of charge to any library that wishes to use it, from <http://tilt.lib.utsystem.edu/resources/index.html>.

TODAY'S CHALLENGES

Once an information literacy course is established, the work is not over. We address a list of issues: increased demand for reference, maintenance of the course, recruiting and training teachers, retention, and assessment. Helping students access LIB111 and related resources is an ongoing challenge. At times during the semester the SLN Web server, the UCCC campus server, Internet service provider or any of the many servers of our database vendors may be down. The technical support staff maintaining each of these servers will claim, probably accurately, that it is available 99% of the time or more. But they are not all available the same 99% of the time. Maintenance of the course is also ongoing. New resources become available; links to existing resources change.

UCCC librarians, full-time faculty, and adjunct faculty teach LIB111. Adjunct faculty may be recruited from academic departments at UCCC or elsewhere, professionals from UCCC administrative departments, or librarians from other libraries. Recruiting and training teachers will be more difficult next semester. Tutors, counselors, librarians, and adjunct faculty were lost this year as a result of the large budget shortfall at UCCC.

Faculty who teach LIB111 online must attend Faculty Development Workshops offered by SLN on SUNY campuses at regional locations across the state. Teachers are given lunch by SLN and reimbursed for their mileage by UCCC but do not receive any additional compensation for attending the training sessions. LIB111, like all SLN courses, runs on Lotus Notes™. Teachers receive basic training on Lotus Notes™ and instructional design during the three training sessions. Each teacher receives a Lotus Notes™ manual and the *SLN Course Developer's Handbook* to take home. Each participating college is also assigned an instructional design partner or MID, either on campus or available by phone or e-mail.

Librarians at UCCC continue to work to integrate information literacy competencies throughout the curriculum. The National Survey of Information Technology in U.S. Higher Education (1999) identifies "assisting faculty efforts to integrate IT into instruction" (National survey 1) as the single most important IT challenge confronting American colleges and universities. The LIB111 project has opened an avenue for collaboration between librarians and teaching faculty. At UCCC "there are faculty members teaching LIB111, changing the other courses they teach as a direct result of the experience, and inspiring their colleagues to do the same" (Berk 1).

RETENTION

While retention is a college-wide concern for UCCC as a whole and instructors in all subject areas are aware of the need to attract and hold students, retention has become a particular issue for some of the instructors teaching the same course both in the classroom and online. Several of the teachers who teach LIB111 both in the classroom and online have been able to compare the two and see a higher dropout rate in their online classes. This is consistent with findings elsewhere. Some colleges report that fewer than 50 percent of distance education students finish their courses (Carr A39).

Informally questioning individual students indicates a variety of reasons that students fail to complete the online course. The three most common problems appear to be:

- *Poor time management skills.* Students wait until three to five days, or longer, after the course starts to logon for the first time. In contrast, few students intentionally skip the first meetings of a classroom course. Students logon infrequently and for short periods of time–they work on the course "in their spare time" not reserving time for the work. Some students even log on for the first time just before the class ends.

- *Misconceptions about distance education.* Occasionally, students who do not own a computer and cannot get access to a computer, inexplicably, register for the online course. Registered students discard the Library's "Welcome" letter without reading it. Students say that they registered for the online course believing it would be easier and require less work than the same course taken in the classroom. Students ignore the posted course start and end dates and the statement that class participation is required. Many students do not complete the self-administered quiz that UCCC offers to potential distance learners: "Will You Be Successful in an Online Learning Course or Program?" at <http://www.sunyulster.edu/programs/will_you_be_successful.asp>. More than one student has complained that instructors do not reply to their e-mail 24-7.

- *Problems with the technology.* Students are frustrated when the half hour that they have allocated to work on the course is eaten by technical problems. At Georgia State University, Mary Ann Hindes sent over 650 e-mail messages related to the Web-based course that she was teaching and 80 percent of the messages dealt with technical questions and issues (Hindes 97). Students who have never used a computer before, even for e-mail, seem to think that LIB111 might be a good way to learn to use a computer. UCCC does offer computer courses for beginners but LIB111 is not one of them, nor is it described that way in the catalog or at the SLN Web site.

Teachers at UCCC are reporting the high use of distance education options by students who live near the campus. Students are taking advantage of the asynchronous nature of the courses to "time shift" courses because they work or because they cannot get childcare. The responsibilities that fill their schedules are no different from the responsibilities of the students who enroll in classroom courses; however, the scheduling problems that led them to register for distance education may also prevent them from devoting adequate time to their online courses.

A study conducted by Byron W. Brown (available online at http://www. msu.edu/~brownb/vstudy.htm) found that online students tend to spend less time studying than students in a classroom course. Half of the distance education students who participated in the study reported that they spent zero to three hours a week on the course. About 80 percent of the students in the traditional sections spent more than that just attending the class (Carnevale A38).

Sherry Chisamore, who teaches both SLN LIB111 and ENG 102 courses at UCCC, has suggested that the optional "Will You Be Successful in an Online Learning Course or Program?" quiz be improved and required before a student registers for LIB111. Students who are aware that online courses are not less work than the same course given in the classroom will be better prepared to succeed.

At the Manheim Township Virtual High School, in the pre-course survey, all of the students indicated that they possessed the maturity and discipline to succeed in the courses, and most grade point averages were above 3.2. At the end of the semester, these same students indicated that they lacked the self-discipline to commit the necessary time and energy to attain success in their online courses (Oblender 43). The solution at Manheim is a hybrid combining the Web-based format and the traditional classroom format. At Manheim, the students meet in a computer lab with their teacher directing the Web-based course as a facilitator. Instructors are discussing the use of the hybrid format at UCCC by offering sections of LIB111 with only one or, at most, two classroom meetings, or requiring students to meet with the instructor individually by appointment.

At Concord University School of Law, Dean Martha Siegel says that they "collect data about which students have begun their courses, when they've logged on, how long they've been online, and basically what they've done while there." Students log on to their courses through a personal Web page that includes a color bar for each course the student is enrolled in. When progress in a course is on schedule, the bar is gray. Students who are ahead get a green bar and those who are behind get a red bar. In spite of this close monitoring, Dean Siegel discovered two weeks into a course that 15 to 20 students had not started working. Her solution was to e-mail all students who had not logged on and ask them if they were having problems. "Are you having problems, do you need technical help, I'm here to help and so are others" (Ellis 52). At UCCC we do not monitor students that closely but we can determine that students are not participating and send them e-mail. LIB111 instructor Pepper Boetcker has found that e-mail sent to students who had not participated during the first week of the semester received the best response. LIB111 instructors also have access to student's phone numbers because, if students are having technical problems, e-mail may not reach them.

Assessment, in the general meaning of the word, has been part of LIB111 since the beginning in the form of homework assignments, mid-term, final exam and student survey. But this semester the library was directed to participate in the preparation of a General Education Assessment Plan for Ulster County Community College. SUNY General Education Assessment Review (GEAR) has identified ten general education knowledge and skills areas and two competencies to be addressed over the next three years. Information literacy falls under the Critical Thinking and Information Management competency. Assessment strategy for GEAR is not to determine the individual student's grade, but to improve the quality and quantity of learning in the course. The UCCC GEAR task force had already determined that a course-embedded approach to assessment that would utilize pre-existing course assessment tools such as tests, lab reports, papers, portfolios and performances would be the most efficient. Various assessment models were reviewed and a model based on the Nassau Community College goals-based assessment plan was developed.

In the past assessment plans, the Director of Curriculum, Program Development and Evaluation has prepared reports in collaboration with one or two department chairs. Faculty was generally not involved in the preparation of assessment plans for individual courses. The preparation of the General Education Assessment Plan marks the first time that all faculty members will be involved in a campus-wide assessment program. LIB111 faculty has just started the process. The plan includes a timetable to complete the process on a three-year cycle and information literacy is to be assessed during the 2003-2004 school year.

THE FUTURE OF LIB111 AT UCCC

Distance learning at UCCC will continue to evolve and it is impossible to say at this point whether our five-year plan will turn out to be fact or fiction. Two coming changes in campus technology will impact the future of LIB111: adoption of Ex Libris' ALEPH Integrated Library System to replace our current system, and CollegisEduprise support of World Wide Web Course Tools (WebCT).

With the new Ex Libris system the Macdonald DeWitt Library will have the option of purchasing MetaLib. MetaLib includes ResourceStore–a catalog of the library's electronic databases and resources that provides an organized and searchable list of databases, including collection descriptions and scope–to guide users to the most relevant sources. MetaLib includes SFX (derived from "special effects") to guide users to the institution's preferred sources. With SFX, a library can define rules that allow SFX to dynamically create links that fully integrate the library's information resources regardless of who hosts them–the library itself or external information providers. SFX permits context-sensitive linking among all parts of an electronic collection, including full-text repositories; abstracting, indexing, and citation databases; online library catalogs; and citations appearing in research articles and other Web resources. Even before these options are available to us, LIB111 instructors will be putting even more emphasis on research concepts, flexibility and critical thinking over training to use a specific research tool. LIB111 will have been redesigned to include them by the time these services are actually available.

Currently, the library is offering LIB111 only through the SUNY Learning Network but, at some point, the library may present one or more sections of the course in WebCT. Until recently, however, WebCT did not offer tools for student/teacher interaction equal to those available to users of the SLN using Lotus Notes™. The new version of WebCT offers the Dropbox Management Tool, with a more streamlined method for students to submit their work and several other features that make it easier for instructors to track and grade the assignments. The recently released Campus edition of WebCT also offers student access to administrative services, WebCT courses, and integration with Campus Pipeline and other campus intranet offerings though a single logon. Perhaps the biggest advantage is that WebCT eliminates the need for instructors to use third-party software to make changes in their courses. Editing courses through a Web-based interface allows instructors to make course changes from any networked computer, making it unnecessary to install third-party software like Lotus Notes™ on every computer used to access the course material.

Distance education has seen dramatic growth since LIB111 went online in 1997. During the 1997-1998 school year, LIB111 was one of only 180 courses offered through SLN. In the 2000-2001 school year the number of courses offered through SLN had increased to 1,500. Currently seven online sections of LIB111 are being offered at UCCC. New instructors are eager to participate in distance education because it broadens their experience and makes them more valuable to the college. Instructors who have been teaching online see that both the course management tools and the delivery systems are improving. The growth of the Information Literacy Program at UCCC, both in the classroom and online, has been made possible by the support of the administration, the participation of librarians as information specialists, and the faculty partnerships that have been formed.

WORKS CITED

Berk, Larry. "The Library, Information Literacy, and Campus Politics." A speech given to the Association of College & Research Libraries/Eastern New York. October 13, 1995.

Berk, Larry and Patricia Carroll-Mathes. "Implementation of Information Literacy." *"LOEX" of the West: Collaboration and Instructional Design in a Virtual Environment*. Ed. Kari J. Anderson. Stamford, CT: JAI Press Inc., 1999. 75-83.

Carnevale, Dan. "Online students don't fare as well as classroom counterparts, study finds." *The Chronicle of Higher Education.* 15 March 2002: A38.

Carr, Sarah. "As distance education comes of age, the challenge is keeping the students." *Chronicle of Higher Education.* 11 Feb 2000: A39.

Donnelly, Kimberley M. "Learning from the teaching libraries." *American Libraries.* 29.11 (Dec. 1998): 47.

Ellis, Kristine. "A model class." *Training.* 37.12 (Dec 2000): 50-7. *WilsonSelectPlus* 12 March 2002 <http://firstsearch.oclc.org/>.

Hindes, Mary Ann. "Can Web-based instruction foster information literacy?" *School Libraries World Wide.* 6.2 (July 2000): 88-101. *WilsonSelectPlus* 12 March 2002 <http://firstsearch.oclc.org/>.

Information Literacy Competency Standards for Higher Education. 2000. (12 March 2002 <http://www.ala.org/acrl/ilcomstan.html>).

List, Carla. *Introduction to Information Research.* 2nd edition. Dubuque, Iowa: Kendall/Hunt Publishing Company, 1994.

National Survey of Information Technology in U.S. Higher Education (1999). The Continuing Challenge of Instructional Integration and User Support, *The Campus Computing Project,* <http://www.campuscomputing.net/summaries/1999/index.html>.

Oblender, Thomas E. "A hybrid course model: one solution to the high online drop-out rate." *Learning & Leading with Technology.* 29.6 (March 2002): 42-46.

State University of New York, Office of Information Services. http://olis.sysadm. suny.edu/default9.asp. TILT. University of Texas at Austin.12 March 2002 <http:// tilt.lib.utsystem.edu>.

State University of New York Web-Based Information Literacy Course Request for Proposals. Office of Library and Information Services, State University of New York. April 27, 1999. 12 March 2002. <http://www.sunyconnect.suny.edu/ili/ILRFP.doc>.

Implications of Culture
in Distance Education

Cecilia Salvatore

SUMMARY. As technology for distance education continues to advance, new and different ways of delivering instruction are developed which compel new and different pedagogy for distance education. These in turn compel new studies and research. One area of study is the place of culture in distance education. The ways in which cultural factors shape interaction and perceptions in distance education are described. These provide librarians and other information professionals with further understanding about distance education and its implications to their work. In having this understanding, librarians and information professionals will be better situated for developing and implementing library and information services to instructors, administrators, and student participants in distance education. *[Article copies available for a fee from The Haworth Document Delivery Service: 1-800-HAWORTH. E-mail address: <getinfo@haworthpressinc.com> Website: <http://www.HaworthPress.com> © 2002 by The Haworth Press, Inc. All rights reserved.]*

KEYWORDS. Distance learning, culture and education, virtual reference services

INTRODUCTION

Distance education has become almost a common component of education, particularly in higher education and corporate training. This increase in dis-

Cecilia Salvatore is Assistant Professor, School of Library and Information Management, Emporia State University (E-mail: Salvatoc@esumail.emporia.edu).

[Haworth co-indexing entry note]: "Implications of Culture in Distance Education." Salvatore, Cecilia. Co-published simultaneously in *The Reference Librarian* (The Haworth Information Press, an imprint of The Haworth Press, Inc.) No. 77, 2002, pp. 107-119; and: *Distance Learning: Information Access and Services for Virtual Users* (ed: Hemalata Iyer) The Haworth Information Press, an imprint of The Haworth Press, Inc., 2002, pp. 107-119. Single or multiple copies of this article are available for a fee from The Haworth Document Delivery Service [1-800-HAWORTH, 9:00 a.m. - 5:00 p.m. (EST). E-mail address: getinfo@haworthpressinc. com].

tance education naturally facilitates interest in the ways to utilize it more effectively and efficiently. The current research in distance education is vast and runs the gamut from the study of the use of distance education technology and courseware to the study of the pedagogical implications of distance education. Distance education challenges scholars and researchers, for it encompasses a broad realm of complex issues. These issues include those relevant to the complex nature of participants in distance education, including students and instructors, and to the changes in technology. As technology for distance education continues to advance, new and different ways of delivering instruction are developed which compel new and different pedagogy for distance education. These in turn compel new studies and research. Therefore, in spite of the vast literature on distance education, there's still much more to be learned about this subject.

For librarians and other information professionals, there is much at stake in the research in distance education. Library services have traditionally been provided from a stationary point. This has been facilitated by the traditional approach to delivering instruction–i.e., the delivery of instruction in a classroom on a campus setting. As students go to a campus to attend a class, they are also lured to the library where they receive library and information services.

As distance education changes the delivery of instruction, librarians and information professionals must rethink the way they provide library and information services. In order to do this, they must have a clearer grasp of the complex issues that accompany distance education. Distance learners bring to the learning environment various factors that are inherent to their complex human nature. Additionally, various factors shape the interactions that take place in this learning environment.

Interaction and communication studies have referred to cognitive, affective, linguistic, physical, and cultural factors as shaping interactions and communication processes. In this paper, I intend to show that cultural factors, indeed, shape interactions as well as perceptions in distance education, and hence these factors, and culture as a whole, have a place in the study of distance education. My goal in describing the place of culture in distance education is to provide librarians and other information professionals with further understanding about distance education and its implications to their work. In having this understanding, librarians and information professionals will be better situated for developing and implementing library and information services to instructors, administrators, and student participants in distance education.

METHODOLOGY

The methodology used in this paper is informal analysis of discourse in four classes at a Midwestern university library and information science school. Analyzing discourse here is analyzing text in journal assignments and e-mail communication. Schriffrin posits that discourse is both the structure and function of language.[1] On the other hand, Dell Hymes proposes that discourse is language performance and language enactment.[2] In analyzing discourse here, I focus on the meaning of discourse not just as revealed in the structure of sentences and paragraphs, but as revealed in the context in which these sentences and paragraphs are created and written–and hence, in the function of these sentences and paragraphs. In doing this, I look at discourse in these journals and e-mail as the forum in which the culture of the distance education participants is performed and enacted. Hence, in these journals and e-mail, culture is made explicit.

It should be pointed out that I was a participant observer in these classroom environments. The way in which my role shapes the data collection and analysis is not determined. Nevertheless, the findings and descriptions from this research are significant, for they set the stage for further and more systematic research.

BACKGROUND OF RESEARCH LOCUS

The locus of this research is a library and information science school at a university in a state in the Midwest. Since 1988 this school has delivered its curriculum to students in the home state, as well as to distance students in eight other states. In this study, I specifically focus on four classes of students–one held in the home state, two others held at distance sites, and one held at another location in which both the home state and the distance sites are equally represented. Delivery of instruction was made in three formats: (1) in face-to-face meetings between the instructor and students during one weekend, continued by meetings via the Web, using Web-based courseware; (2) in face-to-face meetings between the instructor and students during two weekends; and (3) via videoconferencing technology for two-three hours around roughly every two weeks, supplemented by the use of Web-based courseware.

It is noteworthy that while students can take classes where they meet physically and face-to-face with their instructor, because for the most part students do not always physically go to the home institution to attend classes, the curriculum offered at this school of library and information science is in many ways a distance education curriculum. And even though in some classes, the instructor comes and meets face-to-face with the class for one or two weekends, ongoing interaction with the instructor, as well as student-student interaction continues by e-mail or via Web-based courseware, as part of classroom discussion or as part of real assignments to be completed. There is a genuine time and space separation between instructor and students, especially as instructors do not set office hours during which students can easily come to meet with him or her.

It is noteworthy that, at this school, distance education is a phenomenon that continues to change just as quickly as the software and technology necessary to provide this education change. To be sure, the school has been innovative in applying emergent distance education software and technology to its delivery of instruction to students at the various sites. Furthermore, the school has been innovative in developing a personnel structure that is more suited to meeting the challenges of distance education. For instance, a notably significant component of the school's distance education program is the presence of a distance coordinator at each distance site. The coordinator serves as the liaison between the "home" site and the students, and provides academic, personal, and social services to students at the site. The coordinators, for example, arrange for students to network with professional associations in their area, as well as for informal social gatherings that aid in the development of a cohesive group.

DEFINITION OF DISTANCE EDUCATION

Distance education suggests that education takes place at a distance. In fact, in the definitions provided by various scholars, the underlying theme is the relationship between education and the concepts of time and space. Perraton, for example, states that distance education is "an educational process in which a significant proportion of the teaching is conducted by someone removed in space and/or time from the learner."[3] Similarly, Moore suggests that distance education is a "concept describing the universe of teacher-learner relationships that exist when learners and instructors are separated by space and/or by time."[4] Moore, furthermore, states, "this universe of relationships can be ordered into a typology that is shaped around the most elementary constructs of the field–namely, the structure of instructional programmes, the interaction between learners and teachers, and the nature and degree of self-directedness of the learner."[5] There are four levels of distance education, according to Moore.[6] There are: distance learning program (this is a program within a university that offers traditional classroom instruction), distance learning unit (this is a separate unit within a system that focuses on distance education), distance learning institution (this is an institution whose sole purpose is to offer distance education), and distance learning consortia (this is when two or more institutions or units share in either the design or delivery of programs, or both).

CULTURE IN DISTANCE EDUCATION

In studies of distance education and distance learning, much attention is given to the learning styles and preferences of students, as well as to the formats and technologies for delivering distance education.[7] In this paper, the focus is on the interactions that take place in the distance learning environment. Interaction and communication studies have referred to cognitive, affective, linguistic, physical, and cultural factors as shaping interactions and communication processes. In this analysis of discourse, two issues begin to emerge as shaping the distance learning environment: (1) community building and the socialization process that allows it, and (2) the establishment of identity. These two issues make explicit the culture of the distance learning environment, and highlight the central place of culture in distance education. Additionally, they make explicit the notion of the subculture and counterculture as inherent components of this culture. According to Martin and Siehl, a subculture exists alongside the dominant culture, while a counterculture exists in defiance of the dominant culture.[8]

The juxtaposition of culture in distance education is a natural one. As Branden and Lambert suggest, distance learning tends to accept cultural difference as the starting point of learning because the heterogeneity of cultures is treated as fact.[9] Hence, culture is central to distance education. Branden and Lambert focus on language and technology as components that make explicit cultural differences in distance education participants. They point out that even though language and technology encourage a global market [and hence, environment], citizens nevertheless strive for individual protective attitudes.[10] These individual protective attitudes include cultural factors.

Definition of Culture

The definition of culture, as Frow and Morris point out, is quite complex and varies according to the discipline in which it is discussed.[11] They suggest that in organization theory, for example, the notion that organizational culture may be reshaped and reworked assumes that culture is a "complex of social customs, values, and expectations that affect our ways of working."[12] Schein, in fact, provides a definition of culture that is widely-accepted in organization theory.[13] He suggests that culture is made explicit in the artifacts found in the organization and in the values and norms and assumptions and beliefs held by members of the organization.[14] On the other hand, Rapport and Overing state that culture is a "system of beliefs, knowledge, values, or sets of practice" that one side of anthropology suggests as part of an "ongoing, creative process," while another side of anthropology suggests as part of a "shared and stable" process.[15]

The descriptions above summarize culture as comprised of beliefs, norms, assumptions, knowledge, values, or sets of practice that are shared and form a system. One can assume, therefore, that in order for one to belong to a particular culture, he or she has to be socialized into the culture. Hence, one who is new to a community has not been socialized into the community, and hence, does not share the culture of the community with other members of that community. However, as Frow and Morris state, "to say that the concept of culture refers to the existence of social groups–their formation, their maintenance, their definition against other groups, the constant process of their re-formation–is to raise difficult questions about the kinds of unity that groups lay claim to."[16] In fact, as stated earlier, while there may be a culture of a community, there may also be subcultures and countercultures within that community. This view underscores the complexity, multiplicity, and constant state of flux of culture.

Community and Identity

Paloff and Pratt suggest that instructors pay particular attention to "a whole new set of physical, emotional, and psychological issues along with the educational issues" that are experienced in distance education.[17] Furthermore, they suggest that instructors should develop ways in which these issues can be resolved so that students have a positive distance learning experience. In this analysis of discourse, the emergence of physical, psychological, and emotional issues in the student experience is clear, as illustrated in the following excerpt in which a student expresses frustration about having to do group work with other students at a distance:

> How are we supposed to work together as a group when one of our group members is having a hard time getting on the Internet? She lives in a very remote part of the state.

Students enrolled in distance education and assigned to work on group projects have varying degrees of technological and communication orientation and capabilities. Distance education can be seen as enabling people to pursue a higher education when they would not do so otherwise. Naturally, this means that distance education can increase the diversity of the student body at a school. Having to adjust to this diversity presents psychological and emotional challenges to students. While, initially, these are psychological and emotional challenges, they ultimately become cultural challenges. In my analysis of discourse, it is revealed that as diverse students begin to share a culture of the class, differences in their technological and communication orientation and capabilities become less pronounced and are less likely to get in the way of their interaction.

Instructors of distance education may turn to group work more so than in traditional classroom settings to facilitate interaction among students. They must be mindful, however, of the fact that this interaction does not always occur easily. In my analysis of discourse, students highlight the problems of group participation to the instructor. In fact, just as instructors stress the importance of group work and group participation, students are quick to identify why and when group work and group participation do not work. This was illustrated in the above excerpt. It is further illustrated in the following:

> We all contributed to the project, except for him. It seemed like he tried to have things his way, and when he failed like that, he disappeared from the group. He wasn't responding to his e-mail and he wasn't posting anything on the discussion forum.

Physical, psychological, and emotional issues are sometimes triggered by lack of cohesiveness among group members. The different groups of students that are the focus of this research are a fruitful focus of research in that they each represent different stages of community building and socialization into a group or community. Students at the distance sites form a cohort and go through the community building process together. However, these cohorts start at different times. Students from one cohort may have just started the program and may not all be socialized into a community, while students from another cohort may be near the end of the program. In fact, as revealed in the analysis, students begin the program with dubious feelings of anxiety as well as feelings of excitement. Not quite halfway into the program, students begin to feel exhausted, as if they have been in the program for quite some time, and yet the end of the route seems so far away.

While this is not unique to distance education and students go through similar group development processes, it is noteworthy that these processes are particularly salient in distance education. In a traditional classroom setting, students go to a physical location to meet with the instructor and with each other, while students in a distance education environment ordinarily do not have a common physical location where they all converge. However, as Paloff and Pratt point out, human nature requires a yearning, a sense of belonging, or a sense of connection to a particular place.[18] Furthermore, as Frow and Morris suggest, particular attention must be paid to at least the components or processes that inevitably make members in a group sense their identity or make members feel part of a coherent "society" or "community."[19]

In the absence of a physical place, community building and the establishment of identity are elements of distance education that make students feel connected to a particular place, albeit not a physical place. The literature suggests that participants in distance education and distance programs feel connected in the notion that they belong to a community. Poole, for example, contends that community building must be an essential component of distance education right from the start, so that in spite of the lack of a common physical place, students can still feel a physical connection to their classmates.[20] Hence, it is clear that community in a distance education environment is one that is not defined by geographical boundaries.

Palloff and Pratt further suggest that instructors of distance education courses must provide an environment that facilitates community building.[21] Examples they give to do this, which are similar to examples given in the rest of the literature, include requiring students to post and share introductory personal essays about themselves. The goal here is to provide a footing for further personal interaction and dialogue that will subsequently establish an online community, which is the online and distance education class.

Students are eager to make public the news that their cohort group culture is formed and easily identifiable. Understandably, therefore, identification with a culture is consistently emphasized, as in the excerpts below:

> We are a good group. We are hard on ourselves, and that's just the way we are.

> So do we have the reputation for being the 'rowdy' ones at the school?

As pointed out earlier, at this school of library and information science, students are aided in the socialization process by the distance coordinators. Distance coordinators are particularly mindful of the notion that students need to feel connected to a place, and hence they provide not just academic and advising services, but personal services as well. Students at the distance sites form cohort groups, supported by the distance coordinators, and hence build their own community. They feel jointly connected to the program even though the "home" site is located in another state. In this program, therefore, the distance coordinators do not leave the socialization process entirely to the faculty and course instructors.

As instructors facilitate community building and the establishment of identity, they should be mindful of the complexity of these processes as they deliver instruction and as they interact with students. Instructors and coordinators can facilitate community building, but they also need to know that students need their own community. Paloff and Pratt suggest that because students in distance education have actively built their community, they feel an empowerment of their role in the learning process and in the class.[22] In fact, a crucial difference between a traditional classroom and a distance, online, or Web-based classroom is that in the former, students default to the faculty for answers to their questions, while in the latter setting, students work with each other and collaboratively and become more involved in their learning.[23]

The separation between the class community and the community of the students only is revealed in the following excerpt:

Student: "You can join us in the chatroom that we started."

Instructor: "Okay. I can find out from the coordinator how I can join."

Student: "This is our chatroom. She doesn't know about it. And we have to invite you to join."

Community building and the establishment of identity and their interrelationship form the complex components of culture in distance education. This complexity is further illustrated in the following excerpt:

> I need to discuss with you the assignments. It was very hard for me to pay attention to your lectures and comments in class. You see, I'm having problems with the people at my site. They make comments about the projects that sometimes confuse me, and sometimes I go home and I don't know which comment is from you and which is from them and what is the difference? There's one person there in particular, in fact, who talks too much in that class, and I don't know what to do about it.

In this example, another layer in the issue of culture in distance education emerges. This is the problem of not being able to decipher and share the culture of the community–i.e., the culture of the particular class. In this example, the student is expressing the problem of feeling that she does not identify herself with the culture of the class. The student was enrolled in a videoconferencing class. She and several other students attend the class at a site, where they are connected to the instructor by audio and video only. While it is important to be mindful of the rituals, rules, and norms that are shared by a community of students enrolled in a distance education class or program, it is equally important to be mindful of the way other students–i.e., the outliers–counter these components of culture. Furthermore, while one may feel that he or she has defined the culture of the community or the group, he or she should look out for subcultures and countercultures that may exist in this community. It is important, therefore, to be wary of assumptions about a culture and public statements about a culture that may not be completely true. As stated earlier, culture has been described as, on the one hand, a stable system, and on the other hand, as a continually negotiated system. Thus, in the dispersed setting of distance education, instructors must approach their classes with great flexibility and be mindful of changes that can happen in these classes.

IMPLICATIONS FOR LIBRARIANS
AND INFORMATION PROFESSIONALS

As distance education has become a firm fixture in education, particularly higher education, librarians and information professionals need to rethink the way they provide library and information services. To be sure, librarians have looked at the place of libraries in distance education: they have looked at methods and practices that are useful for libraries to accommodate distance education and have looked at issues that are important to describing the place of libraries in distance education.

As technology has facilitated the development of distance education, librarians and library administrators have used technology to change the way they provide library and information services. To be sure, libraries have done their part to integrate technology into the way they provide services. Reference services that include e-mail reference services, for example, are now regular services offered at some libraries. In addition, there is currently much discussion about virtual reference services. Yet the technology that exists for the provision of distance education is not always amenable to the provision of reference services. There is interactive technology, for example, such as those used in chats and discussion forums, that have become a standard component of Web courseware, such as WebCT. As Coffman points out, the interactive courseware is good for mimicking classroom settings, but is not good for one-on-one reference sessions. Furthermore, current software does not allow the librarian to guide a person through a database search, or escort them around the Web, as he or she might want to do in a reference session.[24]

Coffman maintains that this will change, however. Advanced technology and the accessibility of information resources and distance education combine to challenge the way library and information services are being provided, so that librarians and library administrators will see to it that the technology for library services is in sync with the technology that embraces distance education. Coffman even suggests that the complete and direct replacement of traditional library services, in which patrons are expected to come to the library's physical location to ask for services, will, in fact, take place. He points to events that already exist which are paving the way for this replacement. He raised, as an example of this, the movement of some accreditation agencies to drop library requirements altogether.

Nevertheless, librarians continue to seek ways in which they can provide equitable services for all students regardless of whether they regularly come to the campus for these services or they access these services as distance education students. The Association of College and Research Libraries, for example, has provided some guidelines that are intended to serve as a framework for providing library and information services to distance education patrons.[25] These guidelines provide useful steps in a multitude of areas, such as finances, management, personnel, facilities, and services. One area, for example, urges a separate funding category and additional staff specifically for distance education and the provision of library and information services to those involved in this type of education. Another area urges that librarians and library administrators must participate in the development of distance programs so that they become involved in the student learning experience from the start. The guidelines adopted by the ACRL help to ensure the central place of libraries in the changing face of higher education.

Beagle, in fact, reviewed the literature relating to distance education to find out the place of libraries in distance education, and found that libraries have been marginalized so that instructors, scholars, and researchers have not made it the focus of the learning environment.[26] Instructors of distance education classes, for example, provide readings for students so that it would not be necessary for these students to use the services of the library. Furthermore, the use of library services is not a function that is integrated in Web-based courseware that is used by instructors of distance education.

This is not to suggest, however, that everyone is happy with this scenario. In fact, Beagle points out that even in this environment, there are students in distance education who wish for the expansion of the library and information services that they get. For example, rather than just receiving the reading material for a class from the instructor, they also want the opportunity to find out more about subject matters discussed in class and therefore, need to use the resources at their libraries. Hence, while it may seem that library services have been marginalized in the distance education literature and in the distance education environment, they can, nevertheless, contribute much to the learning process.

As stated earlier, in this paper I intend to show the place of culture in distance education. As pointed out in this paper, culture has a central place in distance education. But what does this mean for library services? As described above, one of the guidelines provided by ACRL suggests that librarians and library administrators prepare a profile of the distance learning community and its needs. In describing the culture of distance education students and communities we see a glimpse of this profile. We see the importance of community building and the establishment of identity as forming a cultural component in the distance education environment. Hence, as libraries seek to integrate technology into the way they provide services to distance education participants, as libraries look at methods and practices that are useful for libraries to accommodate distance education, and as libraries seek to ensure that their place in higher education is not marginalized, they can look at community building and identity establishment as important cultural issues to pay particular attention to.

NOTES

1. Schriffin, Deborah. *Approaches to Discourse.* (Oxford, UK: Blackwell, 1994).

2. Hymes, Dell. "Models of the Interaction of Language and Social Life," in *Directions in Sociolinguistics: The Ethnography of Communication*, eds. John J. Gumperz and Dell Hymes (New York: Holt, Rinehart, and Winston, Inc., 1972), 35-71.

3. Perraton, Hilary. *Open and Distance Learning in the Developing World.* (London: Routledge, 1982), p. 4.

4. Moore, Michael G., "Theory of transactional distance," in *Theoretical Principles of Distance Education*, ed. Desmond Keegan (London; New York: Routledge, 1993), 22-38.

5. Ibid.

6. Moore, Michael G. *Distance Education: A Systems View*. (Belmont, CA: Wadsworth Publishing Company, 1996).

7. Christensen, Edward W., Anakwe, Uzoamaka P., Kessler, Eric H. Receptivity to distance learning: the effect of technology, reputation, constraints, and learning preferences. *Journal of Research on Computing in Education*, 33 (3) (Spring 2001): 263-279.

8. Martin, Joanne and Siehl, Caren. Organizational culture and counterculture: an uneasy symbiosis. *Organizational Dynamics*, Autumn (1983): 52-64.

9. Branden, Jef van den and Lambert, Jose. Cultural issues related to transnational open and distance learning in universities: a European problem? *British Journal of Educational Leadership*, 30 (3) (July 1999): 251-60.

10. Ibid.

11. Frow, John and Morris, Meaghan. "Cultural Studies," in *Handbook of Qualitative Research*, eds. Norman K. Denzin and Yvonna S. Lincoln (Thousand Oaks, CA: Sage Publications, Inc., 2000), 315-346.

12. Ibid, p. 315.

13. Morgan, Gareth. *Images of Organization*. (Thousand Oaks, CA: Sage Publications, Inc., 1997).

14. Schein, Edgar H. *Organizational culture and leadership*. (San Francisco: Jossey-Bass, 1985).

15. Rapport, Nigel and Joanna Overing. *Social and Cultural Anthropology: The Key Concepts*. (London; New York: Routledge, 2000), 94.

16. Frow, John and Morris, Meaghan. "Cultural Studies," in *Handbook of Qualitative Research*, eds. Norman K. Denzin and Yvonna S. Lincoln (Thousand Oaks, CA: Sage Publications, Inc., 2000), 317.

17. Paloff, Rena M. and Pratt, Keith. Building learning communities in cyberspace: effective strategies for the online classroom. (San Francisco: Jossey-Bass Inc., Publishers), 7.

18. Paloff, Rena M. and Pratt, Keith. Building learning communities in cyberspace: effective strategies for the online classroom. (San Francisco: Jossey-Bass Inc., Publishers).

19. Frow, John and Morris, Meaghan. "Cultural Studies," in *Handbook of Qualitative Research*, eds. Norman K. Denzin and Yvonna S. Lincoln (Thousand Oaks, CA: Sage Publications, Inc., 2000), 317.

20. Poole, Dawn M. Student participation in a discussion-oriented online course: a case study. *Journal of Research on Computing in Education*, 33 (3) (Winter 2000): 162-177.

21. Paloff, Rena M. and Pratt, Keith. Building learning communities in cyberspace: effective strategies for the online classroom. (San Francisco: Jossey-Bass Inc., Publishers).

22. Ibid.

23. Leasure, A. Renee, Davis, Lisa, and Thievon, Susan L. Comparison of student outcomes and preferences in a traditional vs. World Wide Web-based baccalaureate nursing research course. *Journal of Nursing Education*, 39 (4) (April 2000): 149-54.

24. Coffman, Steven. Distance education and virtual reference: where are we headed? *Computers in Libraries*, 21(4) (April 2001): 20-25.

25. Guidelines for distance learning library services. *College & Research Libraries News*, 61 (11) (December 2000): 1023-1029.

26. Beagle, Donald. Web-based learning environments: do libraries matter? *College & Research Libraries*, 61 (4) (July 2000): 367-379.

Assessing Outcomes with Nursing Research Assignments and Citation Analysis of Student Bibliographies

Holly Heller-Ross

SUMMARY. What are the library and information research requirements in a typical undergraduate nursing program? Do distance-learning
library services provide undergraduate nursing students with the research materials they require for their academic work? In order to determine how the broad range of reference, instruction, and access services
offered by Feinberg Library at Plattsburgh State University of New York
are used by students, the author reviewed selected nursing course syllabi
for research requirements and the resulting student research bibliographies as an outcome assessment. The review included 441 bibliographic
citations from 78 student research papers from 1998-1999. Results indicated no significant difference between on- and off-campus student bibliography citations with regards to currency, format or number of citations.
Results also indicated that the reviewed undergraduate nursing research

Holly Heller-Ross is Associate Librarian, Feinberg Library, Plattsburgh State University of New York, 2 Draper Ave, Plattsburgh, NY 12901.

The author is grateful for the support provided by: students and faculty in Plattsburgh
State University's nursing program; Marie Laude, Student Research Assistant; re-
search funding from the Eastern New York Chapter of the Association of College &
Research Libraries (ENY/ACRL) Janice Graham Newkirk Research Award; and pro-
fessional development funding provided by Plattsburgh State University's NYS/UUP
Joint Labor-Management IDA program.

[Haworth co-indexing entry note]: "Assessing Outcomes with Nursing Research Assignments and Citation Analysis of Student Bibliographies." Heller-Ross, Holly. Co-published simultaneously in *The Reference
Librarian* (The Haworth Information Press, an imprint of The Haworth Press, Inc.) No. 77, 2002, pp. 121-140;
and: *Distance Learning: Information Access and Services for Virtual Users* (ed: Hemalata Iyer) The Haworth
Information Press, an imprint of The Haworth Press, Inc., 2002, pp. 121-140. Single or multiple copies of this
article are available for a fee from The Haworth Document Delivery Service [1-800-HAWORTH, 9:00 a.m. -
5:00 p.m. (EST). E-mail address: getinfo@haworthpressinc.com].

121

assignments were indeed designed to promote research integration into nursing practice, and that student access to information was sufficient to allow them to complete their academic assignments. *[Article copies available for a fee from The Haworth Document Delivery Service: 1-800-HAWORTH. E-mail address: <getinfo@haworthpressinc.com> Website: <http://www. HaworthPress.com> © 2002 by The Haworth Press, Inc. All rights reserved.]*

KEYWORDS. Distance learning, virtual reference services, reference for nurses, research on needs of students

INTRODUCTION AND STATEMENT OF RESEARCH PROBLEM

The American Nurses' Association (1989) identified the investigative functions of a nurse at various educational levels. The ANA described the functions of nurses at the baccalaureate level as follows: "Reads, interprets, and evaluates research for applicability to nursing practice . . . shares research findings with colleagues." Nursing faculty must design curriculum and assignments that prepare students to effectively carry out these investigative functions. Nursing students must use these learning opportunities to develop and practice the required skills. While access to library and information services cannot guarantee incorporation of literature into student work and clinical practice, it is a critical prerequisite. Changes in library and educational technologies have resulted in an increasing use of electronic databases and Internet sites for health research. Distance-learning programs have further increased this use by bringing academic courses and electronic library collections to students who may never step onto the physical campus. Access to information and information services remains critical for all students, and the institution offering distance-learning programs remains responsible for providing these resources and services.

Plattsburgh State University of New York offers several distance-learning courses, including an RN-BSN degree program for nurses called the Telenursing Program. Library and information services are provided to distance-learning students in the program through flexible and carefully designed combinations of electronically accessible resources, bibliographic instruction sessions, and distance site-library agreements. Web-based courses are additionally supported through library and computing support Web pages and Web-based interactive reference chat. Initial student opinion survey results collected from 1994 through 1997 gave evidence that students used these library services and appreciated their value.

While student opinion surveys provide valuable insights for service assessment, other measurable outcomes are usually required for continued institutional funding, grant proposals and reports, and educational accreditation. In the fall of 1998, the Outreach Information Services Librarian and the Instruction Librarian at Plattsburgh State posted a survey on several electronic lists (including the Bibliographic Instruction List and Off-Campus Library Services List), to collect information from librarians on trends and issues a variety of libraries face in attempting to deliver instruction and services to a growing audience of distance learners. A lack of clearly identified goals and measurable outcomes for distance-learning instruction was noted as a particular concern by several of the survey respondents (Heller-Ross & Kiple, 2000). This information reinforced the thought that further research was needed to assess whether the library services that Plattsburgh State provided were in fact contributing to the desired educational outcomes of the distance-learning program.

The 1998 ACRL Task Force on Academic Library Outcomes Assessment report stated that "Outcomes, as viewed by the Task Force are the ways in which library users are changed as a result of their contact with the library's resources and programs." The report carefully distinguished between input data (measuring library collections and instructional and reference activities), and outcome data (providing evidence of student academic achievement). The report further pointed to the work of Bonnie Gratch Lindauer (1997), which recommended "syllabi analysis; library use/instruction statistics analysis" and "rating of references or bibliographies; portfolio analysis" as good data collection methods for outcomes assessment.

If nursing faculty were requiring students to utilize the research literature in order to prepare them for a nurses "investigative functions," and if students were using library services and resources to "read, interpret, and evaluate research," then student use of library materials would be evident in their coursework. This evidence could be part of an institutional outcome assessment for distance-learning library services support. In 1998, the Outreach Information Services Librarian selected citation analysis as the research methodology that would provide the best objective and specific assessment of student use of literature to complete their course assignments. Nursing faculty research assignments were analyzed as well, to determine the extent to which the assignments in selected courses required use of published literature, and how they may have guided students to appropriate use of resources. Other assessment tools (student surveys, course grading analysis, conversations with students, librarians, nursing faculty) were also occasionally employed to measure student satisfaction and use of library and information services.

RESEARCH CONTEXT FOR CITATION ANALYSIS

Citation studies have long been used to trace the flow of information and establish reputations of individual authors, journals, research institutes, and universities. The underlying premise is that valuable information will be recognized as such by other researchers and included in subsequent published literature. The more frequently an article or book is cited, the more valuable its information must be. Of course, not all citations are positive, but even a negative reference to a work is interpreted as affirming the significance of the work to the field of study. Faculty tenure decision processes invariably include a review of faculty scholarship, and citation analysis is often used to determine the quality of the faculty member's scholarly contributions. Researchers interested in citation analysis as a tool will easily find extensive literature to consult. A subject search for citation analysis on H. W. Wilson Company's Library Literature on OCLC's FirstSearch (1980-November 2001) yielded 644 documents. Research in discipline specific areas is readily available as well, with a search of the nursing literature in CINAHL on SilverPlatter (1999-2001) for citation analysis in the descriptor field yielding 69 records. Only selected examples focused on nursing, distance-learning, or student research are cited here.

Librarians have often used citation analysis to help inform collection development and journal acquisition decisions and to determine core resources in an academic discipline. Most of this research has used published papers, books, and articles for primary research material. Some examples specific to student research and/or distance-learning include Hardesty and Oltmanns' (1989) article on the undergraduate student use of psychology journals, which presents the history of journal title ranking in psychology. The authors report on their study of journal citations from 105 senior psychology theses at two different institutions, concluding that an identifiable core journals list could not be identified from the student papers. Ruddy's (1998) conference paper on the use of citation analysis to investigate journal usage by off-campus graduate students reports an analysis using citations from 100 master's theses, and also concluded that a wide variety of journal titles (565) were cited and no core list of journals was identified in the study.

Most research has concentrated on published literature analysis, using the ISI Citation Indexes, or other bibliographic study techniques to determine what experienced subject experts find to be the most important research information. The results have then been used by librarians to aid in the selection of resources and research indexes, and in the development of research instructional guides. Some researchers in this area have used student work for their focus, including Burton and Chadwick (2000). Their research focused on student preferences for resource material and found that students writing research reports (63% of students surveyed) "preferred sources that were easy to use and easy to find, whether these sources were library-based or Internet-based."

Citation studies have also been used as a tool for comparing library instruction pedagogies, and more recently to identify student information seeking behaviors. One example of a citation study using student research for this purpose is Fescemyer (2000), writing on the research strategies and citations used by students. This article provides a thorough review of the library literature on citation analysis along with citation research findings from undergraduate geography research exam questions. Hovde (2000), in an article focused on student research paper bibliographies and library instruction, analyzed references from 109 freshman English papers to determine whether students used resources suggested by the library instruction sessions. The results showed that students were indeed using the library online catalog and recommended research databases for their coursework. Cornell University librarians have now published two studies of undergraduate student research bibliographies, focused on tracking the proportion of traditional scholarly resources used by students. The studies (Davis & Cohen, 2001 and Davis, 2002) report a decline in scholarly resources cited, and attribute this primarily to the effect of easy access to popular and technical Web resources.

This limited literature review provides ample evidence that citation analysis has a solid history in library research methodologies. Clearly this single method has been used for a broad range of purpose, with several different subject groups, and has been conducted using both published and unpublished and both faculty and student bibliographies as the research study materials. While most statistical analysis requires either large numbers or strikingly different results between data sets in order for the researcher to draw significant conclusions, even small scale uses of statistical research methods can provide benefits for a single institution (ACRL, 1998). The citation study conducted at Plattsburgh State University will be used as only one component of a multifaceted outcome assessment program currently under development.

RESEARCH CONTEXT FOR DISTANCE-LEARNING

Distance-learning or distance-education is generally accepted to mean a teaching/learning experience between instructors and students who are separated by some combination of time and place. Another term for distance-learning students has been off-campus students, as opposed to on-campus learning and on-campus students. Distributed-learning is often defined as a separate mode of instruction more connected to distributed-computing, whereby instructional materials are delivered through computer-based course packages or tutorials, often to on-campus students. Many American universities have defined distance-learning as distinct from a more traditional independent study or correspondence course, in part due to increased reliance on communications technology (compressed video/audio, satellite, or the Internet for example) that provides fast delivery and additional interactivity. Educational and library associations have established standards and guidelines for both library services for distance-learning and the provision of information literacy instruction.

According to the 2000 Association of College & Research Libraries (ACRL) Guidelines for Distance Learning Library Services, "The originating institution is responsible, through its chief administrative officers and governance organizations, for funding and appropriately meeting the information needs of its distance-learning programs in support of their teaching, learning, and research. This support should provide ready and equivalent library service and learning resources to all its students, regardless of location." The ACRL Guidelines also define the association's philosophy and definitions for distance-learning. According to the document, "Distance-learning library services refers to those library services in support of college, university, or other post-secondary courses and programs offered away from a main campus, or in the absence of a traditional campus, and regardless of where credit is given. These courses may be taught in traditional or non-traditional formats or media, may or may not require physical facilities, and may or may not involve live interaction of teachers and students. The phrase is inclusive of courses in all post-secondary programs designated as: extension, extended, off-campus, extended campus, distance, distributed, open, flexible, franchising, virtual, synchronous, or asynchronous." In addition to library association standards, institutional accrediting bodies (such as the Commission on Higher Education Middle States Association and the National League for Nursing), state boards of education, and academic faculty governing bodies also set standards and criteria for library services and quality of instruction. Outcome assessment is therefore part of each institutions responsibility, allowing a determination of whether the educational standards are being met.

Distance-learning students are particularly affected by the transformation of information storage and research access from traditional print to new electronic formats. Information literacy and technology fluency have become key requirements for the successful completion of a university program or continuing education certificate. Specific competencies include fluency in electronic library and information research, electronic mail and file transfers for communication with faculty and classmates, electronic access to academic records and registration, and proficiency in Internet use for course content as well as information research.

Distance learners have been predominantly part-time, adult or returning students; students in professions where continuing education leads to career opportunities or additional licensure (nursing and allied health, education, engineering, business); and students looking for degrees not offered by their local institutions. Web-based distance learning networks and programs, such as the State University of New York's SUNY Learning Network (SLN), the University of Phoenix Online, and Jones International University, offer significant advantages to working adults, disabled or otherwise homebound students, students in rural and remote areas, students in the military or other jobs where assignments require frequent relocations, and incarcerated students. These students are not often well prepared for academic information research, and need a good deal of faculty and librarian guidance as they progress through their classes. A new and very fast-growing group of distance learners are those technologically proficient students who prefer the time-shifting, no-travel-or-dorm-room independence of interactive video, interactive television, or Web courses. Technology proficiency, however, does not mean that these students have information research and critical information evaluation skill levels beyond their adult and returning student classmates.

The current convergence of technological advances, financial constraints, and changing demographics in higher education has continued to nudge many institutions towards piloting or seriously considering distance- and distributed-learning formats. By all accounts, distance-learning programs, courses, and student enrollments will continue to grow rapidly through the next decade (AFT 2001).

RESEARCH CONTEXT FOR DISTANCE-LEARNING LIBRARY SERVICES AT PLATTSBURGH STATE

Plattsburgh State University is located in northern New York State, about 20 miles from the U.S.-Canadian border. Plattsburgh is a state-supported, comprehensive, co-educational institution, accredited by the Middle States Association of Colleges and Schools. Part of the State University of New York (SUNY) system, Plattsburgh offers nearly 60 major fields of study, and has a student population of about 5,800. Plattsburgh first offered distance courses in 1989, and expanded its distance-learning program in 1994 with a five-year, one million-dollar grant from the U.S. Department of Health and Human Services for the establishment of the Telenursing Program, a distance-learning baccalaureate completion program for Associate Degree and Diploma RNs. In 1999, Plattsburgh joined the SUNY Learning Network (SLN), a system-wide asynchronous learning network for Internet-based courses and degrees. The SLN provides SUNY campuses with faculty professional development, course-management software and Internet servers, technical support and help-desk service, and coordinated publicity for distance- and distributed-learning. Plattsburgh telenursing distance-learning classes are now offered using a real-time, two-way interactive, compressed video/audio system (PictureTel), through e-mail distribution/discussion lists, and through the SLN on the World Wide Web. In the fall 2001 semester, Plattsburgh State had 157 students in the Telenursing Program. Plattsburgh also had an additional 206 students enrolled in 19 different SLN classes, and 360 matriculated students at its extension site at the Adirondack Community College in Glens Falls, NY.

Library services were identified as critical from the start of the Telenursing Program, and funding for a part-time outreach librarian was included in the 1994 grant. The Outreach Librarian established the library services program using a distributed approach to facilitate collaborations with librarians at Feinberg Library and at each distance site. Essentially, all traditional library and computing departments added responsibility for working with the Outreach Librarian to provide services for distance-learners. Faculty and staff revised or created procedures and services to provide equitable support. Examples include offsite nursing book collections, a new electronic interlibrary loan form, electronic reserves, online reference chat, home delivery of article photocopies and books, and off-campus database access through a proxy server. Library faculty teach a required one-credit course, "LIB101 Introduction to Library Research," previously described by Carla List (1995), that was revised for delivery through compressed video and then later revised for online delivery. Telenursing students generally use their distance site libraries and reference librarians first and then electronically connect to Feinberg Library for further research or additional reference assistance.

As the distance-learning program changed to include Web courses, the scope of the library services program changed as well. Less emphasis was placed on providing site-based technology, document delivery, and instructional services. More emphasis was placed on optimizing access to online resources through proxy services and full-text databases, electronic reserves, Web-based instructional guides, and e-mail and chat reference support. Again, while access is a critical prerequisite to information resource use, it cannot guarantee information resource use.

METHODOLOGY

A correlational research study, funded in 1998 by the Eastern New York Chapter of the Association of College & Research Libraries (ENY/ACRL) Janice Graham Newkirk Research Award, was designed to investigate nursing student use of the comprehensive library services provided to Plattsburgh State's distance-learners. The research study proposed to collect data on the incorporation of published research literature into student work submitted to fulfill academic course requirements. The Plattsburgh State Committee for the Protection of Human Subjects reviewed the proposal, the primary researcher's credentials, the funding and consent form (Appendix A), and granted an expedited review approval. Human Subjects Research reviews are intended to protect both individuals and the institution from harm and liability. Plattsburgh State's Sponsored Research Office handles these reviews, manages grant funds, and also offers support and guidance for research projects.

Citation study methodology often includes the use of footnotes and lists of references as well as bibliographies. The difference between references, which may be cited several times throughout a work, and a bibliography, which lists resources only once, is a critical difference. Since this study was intended to investigate student use of the literature by number, currency, and type, student research papers with bibliography and works cited sections were used. The purpose was not to establish the importance of the individual referenced materials, nor to identify frequently cited materials, but to determine broad patterns of student use of the published literature. Accordingly, bibliographic citations were counted once, even if cited several times in a research paper.

STUDENT RESEARCH CITATION ANALYSIS METHODOLOGY

Student research participants were recruited from two (NUR 350 and NUR 425) of the Plattsburgh State nursing courses reviewed in the nursing research assignment analysis. Potential participants were given information about the study and were asked to sign a written consent form. Student bibliographies and works cited sections (from research papers, case studies, and group presentations) were collected by photocopying those pages when they were handed in to the course instructors. The bibliographic citations, without any information identifying the student, were then entered into a database of literature consulted by students in the program. This database was constructed to organize the citations according to the following resource characteristics: the number of different research sources consulted, currency of resources consulted, and the format of resources consulted (books, journals, media, Web resources). For purposes of this study, citations from full-text article databases were counted as journals, and not as Web resources. The research findings were reviewed and analyzed for statistically significant differences between on- and off-campus student use of the research literature, as well as for patterns of resource characteristics.

Findings were further reviewed for possible relevance to various questions of interest to the library and nursing faculty. Are students able to locate resources as required by their course assignments? What is the impact of library instruction on student use of resources? Do students without access to Plattsburgh

State's physical library use online resources more than on-campus students do? Are books still utilized by students in their research? Of course, some of these questions can only be answered through consideration of multiple issues, but it was hoped that the research findings would contribute to the ability of librarians to formulate the answers.

NURSING RESEARCH ASSIGNMENT ANALYSIS METHODOLOGY

Nursing research assignments were analyzed in order to determine student research requirements and faculty exxpectations for student research. It is commonly accepted that faculty requirements, and not inherent student love of learning, most strongly influence the amount of research undergraduates pursue for course assignments. Nursing research assignments in four classes offered through distance learning were reviewed for their specific library and information research requirements.

Analysis included review for specifics of length of assignment, guidelines for references or bibliographies, resource currency or format requirements or restrictions, and for the importance of the research assignment in the course grading structure (percentage of the total grade). This analysis was intended to inform the student citation analysis in several ways. If the nursing research assignments primarily required the use of journal articles, then significant student use of journal articles could not necessarily be interpreted as a student preference for journal articles. If the nursing research requirements restricted use of older resources or Web resources, then limited student use of these resources could not necessarily be interpreted as an instructional concern or a resource access issue. On the other hand, since both on- and off-campus students were participating in the same classes, differences between these two populations could be interpreted as real differences in student knowledge, access or preference. Review of the importance of the assignment in the course grading structure was included in the study as a very preliminary and informal measure of the importance of information literacy skills in the nursing curriculum.

RESULTS FOR STUDENT RESEARCH CITATION ANALYSIS

Seventy-eight student research papers providing 441 bibliographic citations were collected and reviewed from 1998-1999. Early comparisons showed differences between on- and off-campus student research citations, although the small sample sizes precluded definitive conclusions.

NUR 350 Fall 1998 Off-Campus Students

Number of Papers Reviewed	Average Number of References	Currency Average 1998	Currency Average 1996-1997	Currency Average 1993-1995	Currency Average 1992 and earlier	Format Average Book	Format Average Journal Article	Format Average Internet	Format Average Media
26	6.88	1.77	2.15	1.23	1.5	2.35	3.88	0.54	0.12

NUR 350 Fall 1998 On-Campus Students

Number of Papers Reviewed	Average Number of References	Currency Average 1998	Currency Average 1996-1997	Currency Average 1993-1995	Currency Average 1992 and earlier	Format Average Book	Format Average Journal Article	Format Average Internet	Format Average Media
15	8.67	2.13	3.6	1.6	0.53	1.8	5.8	0.87	0.07

NUR 350 Fall 1998 Comparison of Averages

category	# refs	1998	1996-97	1993-95	1992-back	# books	# articles	# Internet	# media
off-campus	6.88	1.77	2.15	1.23	1.5	2.35	3.88	0.54	0.12
on-campus	8.67	2.13	3.6	1.6	0.53	1.8	5.8	0.87	0.07

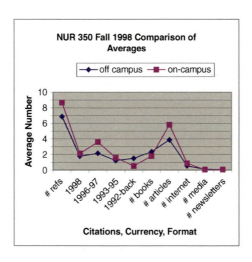

NUR 425 Fall 1998 Off-Campus Students

Number of Papers Reviewed	Average Number of References	Currency Average 1998	Currency Average 1996-1997	Currency Average 1993-1995	Currency Average 1992 and earlier	Format Average Book	Format Average Journal Article	Format Average Internet	Format Average Media
12	4.0	1.16	1.42	0.58	0.83	1.56	0.58	1.08	0.75

NUR 425 Fall 1998 On-Campus Students

Number of Papers Reviewed	Average Number of References	Currency Average 1998	Currency Average 1996-1997	Currency Average 1993-1995	Currency Average 1992 and earlier	Format Average Book	Format Average Journal Article	Format Average Internet	Format Average Media
6	2.66	0.33	1.0	0.83	0.5	1.0	1.16	0.17	0.33

NUR 425 Fall 1998 Comparison of Averages

category	# refs	1998	1996-97	1993-95	1992-back	# books	# articles	# Internet	# media
off-campus	4	1.16	1.42	0.58	0.83	1.56	0.58	1.08	0.75
on-campus	2.66	0.33	1	0.83	0.5	1	1.16	0.17	0.33

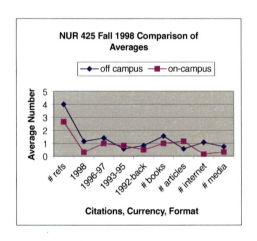

NUR 350 Fall 1999 Combined On- Off-Campus Students

Number of Papers Reviewed	Average Number of References	Currency Average 1999	Currency Average 1998	Currency Average 1996-1997	Currency Average 1993-1995	Currency Average 1992 and earlier	Format Average Book	Format Average Journal Article	Format Average Internet	Format Average Media
19	7.37	2.21	1.68	1.84	0.74	0.74	2.11	4.63	0.58	0.0

NUR 350 Fall 1998 Combined On- Off-Campus Students

Number of Papers Reviewed	Average Number of References	Currency Average 1998	Currency Average 1996-1997	Currency Average 1993-1995	Currency Average 1992 and earlier	Format Average Book	Format Average Journal Article	Format Average Internet	Format Average Media
41	7.54	1.9	2.68	1.37	1.15	2.15	4.59	0.66	0.1

NUR 350 Fall 1998 and Fall 1999 Comparison of Averages

category	# refs	1999	1998	1996-97	1993-95	1992-back	# books	# articles	# Internet	# media
NUR 350 1998	7.54	0	1.9	2.68	1.37	1.15	2.15	4.59	0.66	0.1
NUR 350 1999	7.37	2.21	1.68	1.84	0.74	0.74	2.11	4.63	0.58	0

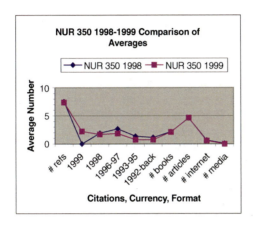

RESULTS FOR NURSING RESEARCH ASSIGNMENT ANALYSIS

Four nursing courses were selected for review in the research study. Two courses (NUR 350 and NUR 425) were reviewed as direct participants in the citation analysis, and two courses (NUR 351 and NUR 437) were selected as part of the core Telenursing Program curriculum. Selected courses were offered to both on- and off-campus students simultaneously, minimizing any potential differences resulting from faculty teaching style or changes in assignment requirements. Course syllabi from 1998/99 were used for the analysis.

Nursing 350 (Theoretical Foundations of Nursing) is a three-credit course covering the essentials of baccalaureate nursing theory and practice. The reviewed research assignment was a traditional term paper covering the presentation of a clinical nursing situation compared to and analyzed against recommendations and practices gathered from a theoretical literature review. The instructor suggested an average length of 10 pages for the paper, and provided fairly detailed guidelines for references. References were to provide a theoretical literature review, include professional journal articles, be sufficiently comprehensive for the nursing topic, and include a minimum number of 5 different sources. This paper was worth 25% of the course grade.

Nursing 351 (Care of Families and the Elderly) is a three-credit course covering trends and factors affecting family health, including health care of the elderly. The reviewed research assignment was similar to the assignment for Nursing 350, a traditional term paper requiring a theoretical literature review. This instructor also recommended a minimum of 5 references, primarily from professional nursing journals, and expected the paper to be approximately 10 pages in length. This paper was worth 25% of the total course grade.

Nursing 425 (Community Health Nursing) is a four-credit course for students in their academic senior year, focused on health care delivery systems and community resources and nursing practices for community wellness. This course includes a clinical nursing component. The reviewed research assignments were a community health assessment paper and a nursing teaching activity presentation. The instructor provided few specific guidelines for the required research materials but very detailed guidelines for the assignment objectives and components. Both assignments required a references list and/or bibliography. Each assignment was worth 15% of the course grade, totaling 30% together.

Nursing 437 (Professional Issues) is a three-credit course also for students in their academic senior year, concentrating on the educational, legal, ethical, political and social issues affecting nursing practice. The reviewed research assignment was a seminar presentation with research, theory, seminar objectives, outlines of policy and legal issues, and seminar discussion questions as required components. The seminar presentation and class discussion were to be lengthy, generally the entire class session. The instructor provided specific guidelines for the research materials; a minimum of 5 current references and professional journal articles were required. The seminar outline and presentation assignment was worth 35% of the course grade.

DISCUSSION AND RECOMMENDATIONS

Comparative analysis of the citation study results shows some difference between the on- and off-campus student groups in their use of the published literature for their course assignments, but not a statistically significant difference. The fall 1998 NUR 350 on-campus students on average cited more references per paper (8.6) than did off-campus students (6.9), and cited more current resources as well. The off-campus students cited an average of 3.88 journal articles, while the on-campus students cited an average of 5.8 journal articles.

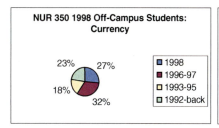

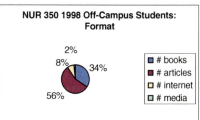

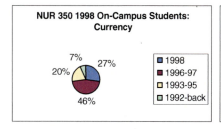

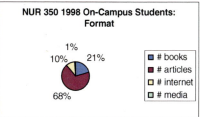

These results suggest differences in research strategies and research decisions between the two groups of students that may serve as indicators for library service and information literacy instructional needs. Follow-up interviews with students may help librarians determine more precisely how students are making their research decisions. Morse and Clintworth (2000) published a research study focused on the effect of format on access to information and student use of biomedical journals. Their results showed that students selected the electronic versions over the print versions ten times more often. Perhaps differences between on- and off-campus student access to fast Internet connections and laser printers for downloading and printing full-text articles contributed to the difference in average number of citations.

The fall 1998 NUR 425 on-campus students on average cited fewer references per paper (2.66) than did off-campus students (4.0), and cited fewer very current resources as well. Off-campus students in this class used more Web resources than did on-campus students, with an average of 1.08 Web citations compared to an average of 0.17 for the on-campus students. These two result sets were opposite patterns from the on- and off-campus averages for NUR 350. The NUR 425 off-campus students cited an average of 0.58 journal articles, while the on-campus students cited an average of 1.16 journal articles. This was a similar pattern to NUR 350.

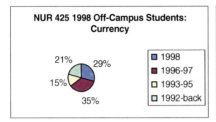

NUR 425 1998 Off-Campus Students: Currency

21%   29%
15%
35%

☐ 1998
■ 1996-97
☐ 1993-95
☐ 1992-back

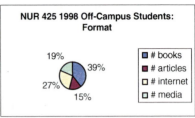

NUR 425 1998 Off-Campus Students: Format

19%   39%
27%
15%

☐ # books
■ # articles
☐ # internet
☐ # media

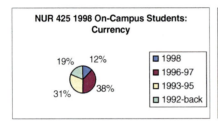

NUR 425 1998 On-Campus Students: Currency

19%   12%
31%   38%

☐ 1998
■ 1996-97
☐ 1993-95
☐ 1992-back

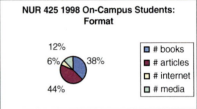

NUR 425 1998 On-Campus Students: Format

12%
6%   38%
44%

☐ # books
■ # articles
☐ # internet
☐ # media

The fall 1999 NUR 350 student data was collected without indication of on- or off-campus status. This data was then compared to a combined on- off-campus student data set from NUR 350 fall 1998. There was very little difference in the average number of citations per paper between the two years, 7.54 in 1998 compared to 7.37 in 1999. There was a similarly small difference in the average currency of the citations, with an average of 1.9 citations from the current year cited by students in the fall 1998 class compared to an average of 2.21 citations from the current year cited by students in the fall 1999 class.

One of the study's early research questions was concerned with whether students without access to the university's physical library use more Web resources. Neither group of students used many Web resources, although access to Web search engines and Web resource guides was provided by Plattsburgh State University. On-campus and off-campus students cited Web resources in similar average numbers for the NUR 350 course (0.87 and 0.54). On-campus NUR 425 students on average cited fewer Web resources (0.17) than did their off-campus classmates (1.08), but the differences were not found to be statistically significant, given the small sample sizes. No restrictions on Web resource use were noted in the written course assignments guidelines, although instructors could have provided oral guidelines for Web use. One possible reason for the minimal use of Web resources is a student concern for reliability, so critical in the medical, nursing and allied health professions.

The second component of the research study was an analysis of course research requirements as an indicator of information literacy importance in the curriculum. Research-based assignments counted as significant portions of each course reviewed in the study. The range of 25-35% certainly points to a strong emphasis on research, analytical and writing skills. This informal measure indicates that the nursing curriculum places a high value on information literacy skills. In keeping with the emphasis placed on research by the American Nurses Association, Plattsburgh nursing faculty require incorporation of research into nursing coursework. This fosters a sense of familiarity with the literature of the nursing profession, and an appreciation for the new information to be gained from consulting published literature.

Instructors sometimes gave specific minimum guidelines for literature resource materials (five references, use of professional journal articles), but also documented expectations of individual student judgment with statements such as "sufficiently comprehensive . . ." guiding students but still requiring critical thinking and professional decision making. Instructors used a variety of assignments, including but not limited to the traditional term paper. This discipline-specific use of the literature could more effectively lead students into regular incorporation of information literacy into nursing practice. Radjenovic and Chally (1998), reporting on their work with undergraduate nursing students on research utilization, wrote "High-quality poster presentations suitable for display at a professional meeting resulted from student efforts . . . ." They also noted that research utilization requires specific evaluation skills and is best if ". . . the research and clinical expertise of faculty members and nursing staff is combined with the developing skills of the undergraduate student." An investigation of the effectiveness of different types of research assignments in preparing nursing students to use published research in their practice would be of great benefit to nursing educators. Few nurses will write formal papers after graduation, although the term paper remains an excellent strategy for developing knowledge in a subject. Many more nurses will prepare teaching activities for patients and their families, prepare and conduct in-service seminars for their colleagues, and assess community health needs and available services. Faculty inclusion of independent literature research in a variety of course assignments contributes to student recognition of the role information literacy skills can play in their future professional nursing practice.

Comparison of the citation study results to the research requirement review indicate that faculty written assignment requirements and assignment type (research paper or teaching activity or seminar presentation) have much more impact on student use of the literature than do any potential differences in access to resources on- or off-campus. The average number of citations for the NUR 350 research paper was 7.54 in 1998 and 7.37 in 1999. The assignment required a minimum of 5 different sources and most students exceeded this requirement. The average number of citations for the NUR 425 teaching activity was 4.0 for off-campus students and 2.66 for on-campus students, many fewer than the average numbers cited for the NUR 350 research paper.

The NUR 350 instructor recommended use of professional journal articles, and students cited more than twice as many journals than books in both 1998 and 1999. There were no specific written guidelines for resource format in the NUR 425 assignment and the citation analysis results showed that students used a more evenly spread selection of books, journals, Internet and media resources than did students in NUR 350. Instructor guidelines clearly bear great weight in student selection and use of resources.

In addition to selecting, organizing and providing access to information resources, in addition to preparing and delivering research instruction and information literacy sessions, this small study indicates that librarians at Plattsburgh State University need to continue to work with departmental faculty as they develop research assignments and research resource guidelines. Closing the loop between providing services and assessing outcomes with small studies such as this one can help point us in the right direction.

REFERENCES

Association of College & Research Libraries (2000). Guidelines for Distance Learning Library Services. Available online from [http://www.ala.org/acrl/guidelines/disl].

ACRL. (1998). Task Force on Academic Library Outcomes Assessment Report. Available online from [http://www.ala.org/acrl/outcome.html].

American Federation of Teachers. (2001). "A Virtual Revolution: Trends in the expansion of distance learning."

Burton, Vicki Tolar, and Chadwick, Scott A. (2000). *Investigating the practices of student researchers: patterns of use and criteria for use of Internet and library sources. Computers and Composition* 17, 309-328.

Davis, Philip M. (2002). *The Effect of the web on undergraduate citation behavior: A 2000 update. College & Research Libraries* 63 (1), 53-60.

Davis, Philip M. and Cohen, Suzanne A. (2001). *The Effect of the web on undergraduate citation behavior 1996-1999. Journal of the American Society for Information Science and Technology* 52, 309-14.

Fescemyer, Kathy. (2000). *Information-seeking behavior of undergraduate geography students. Research Strategies* 17 (4), 307-317.

Hardesty, Larry and Oltmanns, Gail. (1989). *How many psychology journals are enough? A study of the use of psychology journals by undergraduates. The Serials Librarian* 16 (1/2), 133-153.

Heller-Ross, Holly and Kiple, Julia. (2000). *Information Literacy for Interactive Distance Learners. In Teaching the New Library to Today's Users: Reaching International, Minority, Senior Citizen, Gay/Lesbian, First Generation College, At-Risk, Graduate and Returning Students, and Distance Learners,* edited by Trudi E. Jacobson and Helene C. Williams. Neal-Schuman Publishers, Inc.

Hovde, Karen. (2000). *Check the Citation: library instruction and student paper bibliographies. Research Strategies* 17, 3-9.

List, Carla. (1995). *Branching out: A required library research course targets disciplines and programs. The Reference Librarian* 51, 385-398.

Morse, David H. and Clintworth, William A. (2000). *Comparing patterns of print and electronic journal use in an academic health science library. Issues in Science and Technology Librarianship.* Retrieved Online April 12, 2001 at [http://www.library.ucsb.edu/istl/00-fall/refereed.html].

Okrent, Nicholas. (2001). *Use of full-text electronic resources by philosophy students at UNC-Chapel Hill: a citation analysis.* University of North Carolina, Masters Thesis. Retrieved Online November 5, 2001 at [http://ils.unc.edu/Mspapers/2685.pdf].

Ruddy, Margaret. (1998). Using Citation analysis to identify and monitor journal usage by off-campus graduate students (at Cardinal Stritch University). In *The Eighth Off-Campus Library Services Conference Proceedings.* P239-243.

Radjenovic, Doreen and Chally, Pamela S. (1998). *Research Utilization by Undergraduate Students. Nurse Educator* 23 (2) 26-29.

APPENDIX A

Informed Consent
Research Study Participation

Research Project: Incorporation of Published Literature into Student Research: Impact of
Library Services for Distance Learners in the Plattsburgh State
Telenursing RN-BSN Program.
Principal Investigator: Holly Heller-Ross, MLS, Plattsburgh State University

I understand that I am being asked to participate in a bibliography research study to document student use of published literature (books, journal articles, WWW pages, pamphlets) in their academic coursework.

I understand that I am not required to participate in the research study.

I understand that the purpose of this research study is to improve understanding of student research and use of published literature to complete academic assignments in the Telenursing program. A further purpose is to analyze the research results and improve library resources and library instructional activities for Telenursing students. A final purpose is to investigate any differences between resources cited by on and off-campus students.

I understand that my instructor will not be informed of my decision about participating, and that my decision will not affect my course grade in any way.

I understand that a student research assistant for this research study will photocopy the references cited or bibliography section of my academic paper/project. The references cited will then be compiled into a statistical database for analysis and possible publication, and my references will be identified only as an on or off-campus student, and not by name, sex or age.

YES _____   _____
I agree to participate in the bibliography research study (signature)   date

NO _____   _____
I do NOT agree to participate in the bibliography research study (signature)   date

Index

Page numbers followed by f indicate figures.

Academic Dean, 92
AcademicInfo, 34
ACRL. *See* Association of College and
    Research Libraries (ACRL)
ACRL Instruction Section Innovation
    in Instruction Award, 99
Adirondack Community College, 128
Advanced Learning & Information
    Services, 94
Aggarwal, A., 9
ALA. *See* American Library
    Association (ALA)
ALA Standards Committee, 45
ALEPH Integrated Library System,
    103
Aleph500 system, 53
Alexander, A.W., 59
(ADEPT) Alexandria Digital Earth
    Prototype, 68
Alexandria Digital Earth Prototype
    (ADEPT), 68
Allen, B.M., 46,54
AllExperts, 36
ALNs. *See* Asynchronous learning
    networks (ALNs)
AltaVista, 23-24,25
American Council on Education, 45-46
American Library Association (ALA),
    40
American Nurses Association (ANA),
    122,137
ANA. *See* American Nurses
    Association (ANA)
Anderson, T., 14

Andreesen, M., 32
AOL Instant Messenger, 35
AOL Search, 33
Area Studies Component, 43
arXiv, 35
Assessing Digital Library Services, 68
Association of College and Research
    Libraries (ACRL),
    45,94,116-117
Association of College and Research
    Libraries (ACRL) Standards
    and Accreditation Committee
    (SAC), 64
Association of College and Research
    Library (ACRL) Information
    Literacy Standards for Higher
    Education, 91
Association of Research Libraries, 43
Asynchronous learning networks
    (ALNs), 3-17
  access to, 10-11
  community in, 9-14
  cost of, 5-7
    faculty investment in, 6
    financial issues in, 5-6
    technologic factors in, 6-7
  friction in, 13-14
  instructional immediacy in, 11
  instructor role changes in, 12
  learning environment of, 7-9
  peer immediacy in, 12
  social presence in, 12-13
  students' responsibility in, 10
Ault, M., 65

Bangert-Drowns, R.L., 9
Beagle, D., 117
Bellack, 12
Berk, L., 91,93,99
Berners-Lee, T., 32
Bibliography(ies), student
    citation analysis of, assessment of
        outcomes of, 121-139. *See
        also* Citation analysis
    discussion of, 134-138,135f,136f
    methodology in, 128-129
    recommendations for,
        134-138,135f,136f
    nursing research assignments of,
        assessment of outcomes of,
        121-139
BioOne, 44
Bishop, A., 68
Bobish, G., 2,71
Boetcker, R., 97
Books You Teach Every Semester
    (BYTES), 47
Bostwick, S.L., 47,59
Bourne, J.R., 5,9
Branden, J., 111
Bridges, K., 57
Brin, S., 32-33
Brown, B.W., 102
Bruegging, K., 93
Bruner, J., 7
Burton, V.T., 124-125
Bush, V., 31-32,36
Buttenfield, B., 68
BYTES (Books You Teach Every
    Semester), 47

California Digital Library, 35
California State University (CSU), 49
Campbell, G.L., 5,40
Campus Pipeline, 104
Cannon, N., 1,31
CARL, 42
Carr-Chellman, A., 65,66
Carroll-Mathes, P., 91-92,93,94,95,
    97,99

Carter, 68
Casper, 68
CDRS. *See Collaborative Digital
    Reference Service (CDRS)*
Center for Research Libraries (CRL),
    42-43
Central Connecticut State University
    Library, 24
CERN. *See* Conseil Européenne pour
    la Recherche Nucleaire
    (CERN)
CETUS (Consortium for Educational
    Technology for University
    Systems), 49
Chadwick, S.A., 124-125
Chally, P.S., 137
Charnes, A., 43
Chisamore, S., 102
Chu, H., 23
CINAHL, 124
Citation analysis
    research context for, 124-125
    of student biographies, assessment
        of outcomes of, 121-139
    student research
        methodology in, 129-130
        results for, 130,131f-133f
City University of New York (CUNY),
    42,49
Clarkson University, 41
Clearink's Palette Man, 78
Clintworth, W.A., 135
Coffman, S., 116
*Collaborative Digital Reference
    Service (CDRS)*, 35-36
Collaborative Information Literacy
    Project, 94
CollegisEduprise, 97
Commission on Higher Education
    Middle States Association,
    126
Committee on Cooperation in Indexing
    and Cataloguing, 40
Committee on Intellectual
    Cooperation, 40

Community(ies)
  in ALNs, 9-14
  in distance education, 112-115
Computer Industry Almanac, Inc., 72
Concord University School of Law,
  102
Conseil Européenne pour la Recherche
  Nucleaire (CERN), 32
Consortia, in providing direct and
    indirect support for distance
    higher education
  changing role of, 39-62
    introduction to, 40
    problems associated with and
      solutions for, 51-59
    early roles of, 41-44
    types of, growth of, 41-44
Consortium for Educational
    Technology for University
    Systems (CETUS), 49
Consortium of Consortia, 44
Consortium of University Research
    Libraries (CURL), 43
"Consortium-to-consortium (C2C)
    services," 53
Cooper, R., 55,66,67
"Co-operation Versus Competition,"
  40
Cornell University, 35,125
Couperin, 43
Cox, 68
Critical Thinking and Information
    Management, 103
CRL. *See* Center for Research
    Libraries (CRL)
CSU. *See* California State University
    (CSU)
Culture
  defined, 111-112
  in distance education, 107-119. *See*
    also Distance education,
    culture effects on
CUNY. *See* City University of New
    York (CUNY)

CURL (Consortium of University
    Research Libraries), 43
Current Population Survey, 72
Current Serials Component, 43

Dempsey, P., 55,66,67
Dewey, M., 40
DIALOG, 23
Dickinson, D.W., 58
Digital Library Use: Social Practice in
    Design and Evaluation, 68
Distance education
  culture effects on, 107-119
    community in, 112-115
    described, 110-115
    identity in, 112-115
    implications for librarians and
      information professionals,
      115-117
    introduction to, 107-108
    methodology in, 108-109
    research locus in, 109-110
  defined, 110
  instructional services for, 63-70
    distance learners, described,
      66-67
    issues related to, 67-68
    literature review for, 68-69
    locations for, 64-66
    providers of, 66-67
  support for, consortia's role in,
    39-62. *See also* Consortia, in
    providing direct and indirect
    support for distance higher
    education, changing role of
  World Wide Web in, 72-73
Distance learners
  information retrieval on World
    Wide Web by, 19-30. *See*
    also Information retrieval, on
    World Wide Web, distance
    learners and
  instructional services for, 66-67
Distance learning
  research context for, 125-127

at UCCC, 90
Distance learning services, at
    Plattsburgh State University
    of New York, research
    context for, 127-128
Doctor HTML, 82
Donnelly, K.M., 91
Dow Jones Interactive, 23
Dreamweaver, 86
Dropbox Management Tools, 104
Duchastel, P., 65
Duke University, 40
Duke University Libraries, 99

Eastern New York Chapter of the
    Association of College &
    Research Libraries
    (ENY/ACRL) Janice Graham
    Newkirk Research Award,
    128-129
Education, distance. *See also* Distance
    education
    support for, consortia's role in,
        39-62. *See also* Consortia, in
        providing direct and indirect
        support for distance higher
        education
EDUCAUSE, 45-46
Ehrhard, B.J., 56-57
Elsevier ScienceDirect OnSite China
    Corsortium, 43
EmpireLink, 53
Environment, learning, of ALNs, 7-9
ENY/ACRL. *See* Eastern New York
    Chapter of the Association of
    College & Research Libraries
    (ENY/ACRL) Janice Graham
    Newkirk Research Award
ERIC CD-ROM, 55
ERNET, 43
"Error 404–File Not Found," 32
eScholarship program, 35
Ex Libris, 103
Excite, 24
Explorer, 82,86

Faculty Development Workshops, 100
Faloutsos, C., 72
Fein, H., 93
Feinberg Library, 128
    at Plattsburgh State University of
        New York, 121-139
Feldman, S.E., 23
Fescemyer, K., 125
Foreign Doctoral Dissertations
    Component, 43
Fort Drum Consortium, 55
Franklin, B., 46
Frow, J., 11,112,113

GALILEO (Georgia Library Learning
    Online), 42
Garnsey, M.R., 1,19
GEAR (General Education Assessment
    Review), at UCCC, 103
General Education Assessment Review
    (GEAR), at UCCC, 103
Georgia Library Learning Online
    (GALILEO), 42
Georgia State University, 101
Germain, C.A., 2,71
Gerstung, C., 93
GIF (Graphic Interchange Format), 79
Giles, C., 21
Global Newspapers Component, 43
Google, 32,33,34
Gordon, M., 21,22
Gorman, 68
Graphic Interchange Format (GIF), 79
"Grouping of Places for Library
    Purposes," 40
*Guidelines for Distance Learning
    Library Services*, 64
Guidelines for Distance Learning
    Library Services, of ACRL,
    126
*Guidelines for Distance Learning
    Library Services*, 45
*Guidelines for Instruction Programs in
    Academic Libraries*, 64
Gunawardena, C.N., 14

Haresty, L., 124
Hatch, C., 97
Heller-Ross, H., 2,121
HELLIS, 43
Herrmann, F., 13-14
Higher education, distance, support
    for, consortia's role in, 39-62.
    See also Consortia, in
    providing direct and indirect
    support for distance higher
    education, changing role of
Hiltz, S.R., 7,8
Hindes, M.A., 101
Hirshon, A., 46,49
HotBot, 23,33
Hsieh-Yee, I., 23
H.W. Wilson Company's Library
    Literature on OCLC's
    FirstSearch, 124
Hyman, 12
Hymes, D., 109
Hypertext Preprocessor (PHP), 86

ICOLC (International Coalition of
    Library Consortia), 44,52
ILCSO (Illinois Library Computer
    Systems Organization), 42
Illinois Library Computer Systems
    Organization (ILCSO), 42
Individual Studies Program, at UCCC,
    90
INFLIBNET, 43
Infomine, 33,34
"Information Happy Meals," 58
Information literacy, at UCCC,
    89-105. *See also* Ulster
    County Community College
    (UCCC), information literacy at
*Information Literacy Competency
    Standards for Higher
    Education*, 64
Information Literacy Initiative, at
    UCCC, 91

*Information Resources and Library
    Services for Distance
    Learners: A Framework for
    Quality*, 49
*Information Resources and Library
    Services for Distance
    Learners: Statement of
    Principles*, 49-50
Information retrieval, on World Wide
    Web, distance learners and,
    19-30
    introduction to, 20
Infoseek, 24
InfoSpring Digital Library Project, 43
Inger, S., 52
Institute of Museum and Library
    Services, 33
Instructional services, for distance
    education, 63-70. *See also*
    Distance education,
    instructional services for
INTD 150: Library & Internet
    Research, 99
International Coalition of Library
    Consortia (ICOLC), 44,52
Internet
    finding information on, 20-22
    in library instruction, 72. *See also*
        World Wide Web (WWW),
        library instruction via
    search engines on, evaluation of,
        22-25
Internet information, evaluation of,
    25-28
Introduction to Information Research,
    92
Invisible Web, 34-35
Iona College, 91
ISI Citation Indexes, 124
Iyer, H., 2

Janes, 68
Javascripts.com, 86
JAWS for Windows, 97

Jefferson Community College, 55,99
Joint Photographic Experts Group
  (JPEG), 79-80
Jones International University, 127
Jorgensen, D., 1,3
Journal of Academic Librarianship, 59
JPEG (Joint Photographic Experts
  Group), 79-80

Kanuka, H., 14
Kasowitz, A., 56
Katz, 25
Katzowitz, T., 93
Kinder, R., 2,63
Kingston City School District, 93
Kliebard, 12
Kopp, J.J., 40
Kurzweil Omni 3000, 97
Kyrillidou, M., 43,44,59

Lambert, J., 111
LAMDA (London and Manchester
  Document Access), 43
Larabie Fonts, 78
Lawrence, S., 21
Learning environment, of ALNs, 7-9
Leighton, H.V., 24
"LIB101 Introduction to Library
  Research," 128
LIB111, 91,100,101
  at UCCC, future of, 103-104
  on World Wide Web, 93-99
Librarians' Index to the Internet, 33,34
"Library Co-operation," 40
Library Councils, in New York State,
  48
Library instruction, via World Wide
  Web, 71-88. *See also* World
  Wide Web (WWW), library
  instruction via
Library Journal, 40
Library of California, 33
Library of Congress, 41

Library of the University of California,
  Riverside, 33
Library Orientation Exchange
  (LOEX), 91,92
Library Orientation Exchange (LOEX)
  Clearinghouse, 91-92
*Library Outreach, Partnership and
  Distance Education:
  Reference Librarians at the
  Gateway*, 68
Library Products & Services Program,
  53
Library Services Alliance of New
  Mexico, 44
Library Trends, 68
Lindauer, B.G., 123
List, C., 92,128
LOEX. *See* Library Orientation
  Exchange (LOEX)
London and Manchester Document
  Access (LAMDA), 43
Lotus Notes, 94,100,104
Louisiana Library Network, 42
Lowe, C.A., 14
Lycos, 24,33

Mac, E.A., 40
Macdonald DeWitt Library, 91,92,93,
  95,97,103
Mack, K., 97
Manheim Township Virtual High
  School, 102
Manoff, M., 51,57
Mapedit, 79
Martin, J., 111
Martinez, A.M., 22
McMaster, 5
Mehrabian's "concept of immediacy,"
  defined, 13
Melvil Dewey Library, 99
MELVYL, 42,47
Menon, 55
Meola, M., 66
MetaLib, 103

Middle States Association of Colleges
and Schools, 127
Miller, B., 65
Milne Library at SUNY Oneata, 99
Moby Dick, 79
Montgomery, A.L., 72
Montgomery College, 91
Moore, M.G., 110
Morgan, E.L., 51-52
Morkes, J., 77
Morris, M., 11,112,113
Morse, D.H., 135
Mosaic, 32

Nassau Community College, 103
National Center for Education
Statistics (NCES), 73
National Education Association
(NEA), 73
National Electronic Library, 43
National Institutes of Health, 32
National League for Nursing, 126
National Science Foundation (NSF),
35,72
National Survey of Information
Technology in U.S. Higher
Education, 100
NCES. *See* National Center for
Education Statistics (NCES)
NEA. *See* National Education
Association (NEA)
Neeley, L., 56-57
Netscape, 86
Netscape 6.0, 82
Netscape Search, 33
Network Alliance, 43
New York Consortium of Consortia,
52
New York State Library Network, 53
Nielsen, J., 77
Niemi, J.A., 56-57
1998 ACRL Task force on Academic
Library Outcomes
Assessment, 123
NISSAT, 43

Noam, E.M., 48
Notepad, 86
NOTIS Systems PACLink software,
42
NSF. *See* National Science Foundation
(NSF)
Nursing research assignment analysis
methodology in, 130
results for, 133-134
NyLink, 53

OASIS distance education program,
89,90
*Objectives for Information Literacy
Instruction: A Model
Statement for Academic
Librarians*, 64
Oder, N., 52
Office of Library and Information
Services (OLIS), 53
Office of Library and Information
Services(OLIS) Information
Literacy Web-Based Task
Force, of State University of
New York, 95
OHIOLINK, 42
Olson, 9
Oltmanns, G., 124
OPACs, 57
Open Directory Project, 33
Open Publication License (OPL), 86
Open source movement, 33
OpenText, 23
Opera, 86
OPL (Open Publication License), 86
Outreach Information Services
Librarian, 123
"Outreach to Distance Learners: When
the Distance Education
Instructor Sends Students to
the Library, Where Do They
Go?", 68
Overing, J., 111

Packer, 24
Page, L., 32-33
Paloff, R.M., 9,112,113,114
Pathak, P., 21,22
Peifer, E., 93
Perraton, 110
Peters, T.A., 52-53
PHP (Hypertext Preprocessor), 86
PigeonRank, 32
Plattsburgh State Committee for the
        Protection of Human
        Subjects, 129
Plattsburgh State University of New
        York, 125
    distance learning services at,
        research context for, 127-128
    Feinberg Library at, 121-139. *See
        also* Bibliography(ies),
        student, citation analysis of,
        assessment of outcomes of;
        Citation analysis
Poole, D.M., 10,11,12,13,113
PORTALS (Portland Area Library
        System), 42
Portland Area Library System
        (PORTALS), 42
Potter, W.G., 59
Pratt, K., 9,112,113,114
Princeton University, 40
Projectcool Developerzone, 78
Public Libraries, 40
Pyke, C., 9

Queryserver, 34
Quinn, B., 58

Radjenovic, D., 137
Rapport, N., 111
Reader's Guide to Periodicals, 24
Reference librarians, in virtual
        reference services, skills
        needed by, 36

Retrospective Collections Component,
        43
Rettig, J., 25
Rieger, 5
Rosenthal, M., 23
Ruddy, M., 124

Salvatore, C., 2,107
Sanchez, E.F., 22
Saunders, L.M., 54
Schau, T., 72
Schein, E.H., 111
Scholarly Publishing and Academic
        Resources Coalition
        (SPARC), 44
Schrum, L., 12
Science, 48
SCLD. *See* SUNY Council of Library
        Directors (SCLD)
Search Engine Watch award, 33
Search engines, in virtual reference
        services, 32-33
SENYLRC (Southeastern New York
        Library Resources Council),
        93
SFX, 103-104
Shanghai Jiaotong University, 43
Siegel, M., 102
Siehl, C., 111
SilverPlatter, 55,124
Skaar, L., 97
Skinner, B.F., 32-33
SLN Course Developer's Handbook,
        100
SLN Web server, 100
Smith, A.G., 12,25
SO-LINET (Southeastern Library
        Network), 53
Southeastern Library Network
        (SO-LINET), 53
Southeastern New York Library
        Resources Council
        (SENYLRC), 93

SPARC (Scholarly Publishing and
Academic Resources
Coalition), 44
Srivastava, J., 24
St. Lawrence University, 41
Stanford University, 32
State University of New York
(SUNY), 42,49,53,90,127
State University of New York (SUNY)
Office of Library and
Information Services (OLIS)
Information Literacy
Web-Based Task Force, 95
Stormont, S., 66
Student research citation analysis
methodology in, 129-130
results for, 130,131f-133f
Subject directories, in virtual reference
services, 33
Subramanian, J.M., 1,39
SUNY. *See* State University of New
York (SUNY)
Office of Library & Information
Services at, 97
SUNY Canton, 41
SUNY Council of Library Directors
(SCLD), 95,96
SUNY Council of Library Directors
Information Literacy
Committee, 97
SUNY Express, 42
SUNY Information Literacy Initiative
Task Force, 95-96
SUNY Learning Network (SLN),
11,89,90,94,104,127
SUNY Office of Educational
Technology, 93
SUNY Oneida, Milne Library at, 99
SUNY Potsdam, 41
SUNYConnect, 47,48
SUNYConnect initiatives, 53
Swan, K., 11
Swauger, D., 93,95

"Teaching From the Web:
Constructing a Library
Learning Environment Where
Connections Can Be Made,"
68
Teaching/Learning Center, 92,93
Telenursing Program, 55,122,127-128
Texas Information Literacy Tutorial
(TILT), 71,85-86,99
TEXSHARE, 42
The Internet Scout Report, 33
The Reference Librarian, 68
Tillman, H.N., 26
TILT. *See* Texas Information Literacy
Tutorial (TILT)
Tomaiuolo, N.G., 24
Triangle Research Libraries Network,
40
Tsinghua University, 43
2000 Association of College &
Research Libraries (ACRL)
Guidelines for Distance
Learning Library Services,
126
Tyckoson, D., 65

UCCC. *See* Ulster County Community
College (UCCC)
UCCC Information Literacy Project,
94
UKB, 43
ULAKBIM, 43
Ulster County Community College
(UCCC)
distance learning at, 90
General Education Assessment Plan
for, 1-3
information literacy at, 89-105. *See
also* LIB111, on World Wide
Web
challenges related to, 99-100
described, 91-93
future of, 103-104
introduction to, 90

retention of, 100-103
Information Literacy Initiative at,
    91
OASIS program in, 90
site of, 90
Web site, 90
"Universal Library: A Plea for Placing
    Any Desired Book Within the
    Reach of Any Person
    Wishing to Make A
    Reasonable Use of Same," 40
University at Albany, 71,76,81
University at Albany Libraries, 83
University of California, 40
University of Georgia, 27
University of New Mexico, 91
University of North Carolina, 40
University of Oklahoma, 91
University of Phoenix Online, 127
University of Texas, at Austin, 85,86
U.S. Department of Education reports, 4
U.S. Department of Health and Human
    Services, 127
U.S. Office of Education, 40
User Education Department, at
    University of Albany, 71
UTAD (Utah Article Delivery
    Service), 42
Utah Article Delivery Service
    (UTAD), 42

Van House, N., 68
Viagra, 32
VIDYANET, 43
Viggiano, R., 65
Virtual Acquisition Shelf & News, 33
Virtual Library of Virginia (VIVA), 42
Virtual Reference Desk AskA
    Consortium, 56
Virtual reference desks, 34
Virtual reference services
    described, 35-36
    future of, 36
    invisible Web in, 34-35

journal articles related to, 35
    overview of, 31-37
    introduction to, 31-32
    reference librarian skills for, 36
    search engines in, 32-33
    subject directories in, 33
Virtual teaching, 71-88. *See also*
    World Wide Web (WWW),
    library instruction via
VIVA (Virtual Library of Virginia), 42,47
Vivisimo, 33
Vygotskian constructivism, 7

Walsh, R., 2,89
Washington Research Library
    Consortium (WRLC), 42
Web, invisible, 34-35
Web page
    content of, 77
    design of, in library instruction,
        75-76
    physical arrangement of, 77-80,78f,
        79f
WebCT. *See* World Wide Web
    (WWW) Course Tools
    (WebCT)
WebSite Garage, 82
Wegerif, R., 10-11
"Will You Be Successful in an Outline
    Learning Course or
    Program?", 101,102
WILU. *See* Workshop on Instruction in
    Library Use (WILU)
Winona State University Library, 24
Wordpad, 86
Workshop on Instruction in Library
    Use (WILU), 92
World on Paper, 9
World Wide Web (WWW)
    information retrieval on, distance
        learners and, 19-30. *See also*
        Information retrieval, on
        World Wide Web, distance
        learners and

LIB111 on, 93-99. *See also* Ulster
    County Community College
    (UCCC), information literacy
    at library instruction via,
    71-88
  copyright issues related to, 81
  in distance education, 72-73
  evaluation of, 82-85,83f,84f
  goals of, 76-77
  Internet usage in, 72
  introduction to, 72
  literature review related to,
    73-75
  maintenance of, 81
  objectives of, 76-77
  physical arrangement of,
    77-80,78f,79f

    technical issues related to, 80-81
  TILT, 85-86
  usability of, 82
  Web coding tools in, 86-87
  Web page design, 75-76
World Wide Web (WWW)
    Consortium, 43
World Wide Web (WWW) Course
    Tools (WebCT), 103,104,116
WRLC (Washington Research Library
    Consortium), 42
WWW. *See* World Wide Web
    (WWW)

Yahoo, 23